Tales Along El Camino Sierra Two!

David & Gayle Woodruff

El Camino Sierra Publishing
elcaminosierra395@gmail.com
1326 Kimmerling Rd # A
Gardnerville, NV 89460

Copyright© 2019
David & Gayle Woodruff
El Camino Sierra Publishing
All rights reserved

ISBN-978-0-578-46444-2

EL CAMINO SIERRA

EL CAMINO SIERRA
An Aero Conception by Charles Owens, Artist. Reproduced by Courtesy of Los Angeles "Examiner"
Group picture (left to right)—W. G. Scott, Honorable John E. Raker, Professor James F. Chamberlain, N. C. Geary, O. K. Parker, C. E. (kneeling)

El Camino Sierra, "The Mountain Highway," extended from Mojave in Southern California to Lake Tahoe.

The idea of El Camino Sierra began in 1910 as a marketing promotion by the Inyo Good Road Club of Bishop, California, with its purpose…to draw the attention of state legislators to this lightly populated area and obtain a share of the state highway construction funds to build "good roads."

Contents

1.	El Camino Sierra	1
2.	Ferris's Wheel	5
3.	Bishop's Kittie Lee Inn	9
4.	A Jewel of Two States	13
5.	Dunmovin	17
6.	First in Fishing	19
7.	A Natural Scene	21
8.	Fales Hot Springs	25
9.	The Right Thing	29
10.	Reno's First Destination	33
11.	King of the Jungle	37
12.	Tufa Refrigerator of Mono Lake	41
13.	Jailhouse Treasure	43
14.	A Woman to Match the Mountains	45
15.	Minden Heritage	49
16.	Lone Pine Observatory	53
17.	Cold War in the Eastern Sierra	55
18.	Moving Water	57
19.	The Hubcap Queen	61
20.	Lone Pine Stampede	63
21.	Flying Highest	65

CONTENTS

22.	Fremont's Lost Canyon	69
23.	Tex Cushion and His Sled Dogs	71
24.	From the Halls of Pickel Meadows	75
25.	Mint Condition	77
26.	Lady on the Flying Skis	81
27.	Tom's Place	87
28.	Richard Neutra's Oyler House	91
29.	Convict Casino	93
30.	A Sierra Woodpecker	97
31.	Spark Plug	99
32.	Basque of the Eastern Sierra	103
33.	Major Leagues in the High Sierra	109
34.	Hot…Hot…Hot!	111
35.	All Shook Up	115
36.	In It for the Long Run	119
37.	Shrimp Plate?	123
38.	Ghost Riders in the Sky	125
39.	Reno's Levi Legacy	129
40.	Lon Cheney's Cabin	131
41.	Accidental Preservation	133
42.	Chuck Yeager Sierra Stories	139
43.	Springs of Survival	141

Inyo Good Road Club Secretary W.G. Scott (far right) visited California Governor Hiram Johnson (center with straw hat) in Sacramento when the Inyo Good Road Club made a stop in the state capital during the promotional tour of El Camino Sierra-1912

Front Cover-Highway 395 near Washoe Valley and Slide Mountain, Nevada-1930s

Back Cover Photo-El Camino Sierra (Highway 395) near Mono Craters south of Lee Vining, California-1930s

ACKNOWLEDGEMENTS

We are so fortunate to know, and have come to know, so many people who share our own interest and zeal for the land of El Camino Sierra. From friends and family to scholars and fellow historians, literally hundreds of people have contributed in some form, to this written reflection on the area's rich history.

The Eastern Sierra is home to some of the finest small-town museums to be found. All of these repositories of our local and regional heritage have been instrumental in providing us with the needed reference and source material to put together a project such as this. We express so much gratitude to the devoted, tireless and often volunteer staff of these noble treasures. John Klusmire, Roberta Harlan (now retired) and Heather Todd of the Eastern California Museum in Independence, Barbara Moss and Pam Vaughn of Bishop's Laws Museum, Robert Joki and the Southern Mono Historical Society in Mammoth, aka as the Hayden Cabin, David Carle and the Mono Basin Historical Society in Lee Vining, Kent Stoddard and the Mono County Museum in Bridgeport and Gail Allen and the Douglas County Historical Society in Gardnerville, Nevada. Special thanks also to Ray DeLea and his **www.owensvalleyhistory.com.**

Additionally, Florene Trainor and the California Department of Transportation have worked hard to preserve the history of road building in the Eastern Sierra including El Camino Sierra, and have provided volumes of material to us on this uncommon topic. Kat Greenman, Bob Todd, Bill LeFever and Bill Snyder of KSRW radio-the Sierra Wave in Bishop California have supported our work from the start and help keep *Tales Along El Camino Sierra* fresh and relevant with their airing of our radio history program four times a day, seven days a week.

And of course, there is the mundane, tedious and perhaps the most important work of editing, for which we relied heavily on Naiya Luna-Warren of Independence, whose eagle eye and sharp red pencil helped us immeasurably and to whom we are truly grateful.

Last but certainly not least, we thank you our many readers, who have been so gracious to have expressed to us your enjoyment and thoughtful appreciation of our first *Tales Along El Camino Sierra*. Your kind words have formed the foundation of inspiring us to pursue writing this second volume.

El Camino Sierra followed along the base of the wondrous Sierra Nevada Mountains from Mojave in Southern California to sublime Lake Tahoe. Here an early wayfarer stops to take in the stunning scenery of Devil's Gate, a few miles north of Bridgeport.

Travelers were mesmerized from the start by the grandeur of nature found along the route. From the foaming cascades of the Walker River (above) to the imposing Sierra peaks with their fish laden lakes, El Camino Sierra became a prime destination get-away for multitudes of urban dwellers.

A Sentimental Journey

Travel is mostly about dreams—dreaming of landscapes or destinations, imagining yourself in them, murmuring the bewitching place names, and then finding a way to make the dream come true. Escaping to U.S. Highway 395 has been a dream for tens of millions of constrained urban dwellers since word of this magical land was first spread by the inaugural excursionists. A road trip here can become the foundation of the dreams that embolden us to make it through our daily challenges of life.

We have listened to hundreds (if not thousands) of people share their heartfelt reminiscence of their personal Highway 395 experiences. Most expressed their feelings in moving and often emotional reflection. It is clear this iconic roadway has led to the creation of lifelong remembrances with nearly all who have traveled it.

The human history that has transpired along this magical ribbon of blacktop runs as deep as the mountains are high, as captivating as the rivers flow swift. Where else has a Catholic priest been the primary booster of a region's hospitality industry? How many small communities can boast of coalescing so effectively that the world's largest fish hatchery was built in their locale? (both stories in the original *Tales Along El Camino Sierra*).

As the number of visitors coming to this region of grandeur and beauty have increased, so has people's interest in learning more about this fabled and historic realm. *Tales Along El Camino Sierra Two!* brings to life an array of new, seldom told stories from life along El Camino Sierra.

The original Highway 395 auto road got its start at the beginning of the 20th century, shortly after the invention of the first automobile and the highway has played an instrumental role in the milieu of the Eastern Sierra ever since.

Highway 395 was dubbed El Camino Sierra, the Mountain Highway, by its original conceptors before the first roadbed was even graded. These visionaries dreamed of a route that would make travel easier, bring more commerce to the region and unveil to the world the glory that is the Eastern Sierra. Their unbridled enthusiasm and commitment led to the creation of this most favorite of our nation's thoroughfares.

Our own personal lifelong love affair with Highway 395 can be traced back to our early childhoods. With Gayle growing up along the legendary road and David traveling and vacationing along its route since he was old enough to ride in a car, both of us have had a special place in our hearts and minds for this ribbon of blacktop from the start. And incredibly good fortune had befallen upon us when we became permanent Eastern Sierra residents almost thirty years ago.

Over the years, our interest in Eastern Sierra history continued to grow. We discovered a treasure trove of little known and fascinating stories of this epochal region, primarily through extensive research at the Eastern California Museum in Independence, and our passion has only heightened over the years.

We are deeply humbled by the success of our first volume of *Tales Along El Camino Sierra*. We were able to include only 36 stories in the first book and with literally hundreds of tales to be told, it was an easy decision to write this Volume Two.

We hope the factual and often times humorous stories you are about to read will further cement your own personal affaire de Coeur with this iconic highway and the glorious realm it serves.

"The value of history is that it teaches us what man has done and thus what we are"
R. G. Collingwood

CHAPTER ONE

EL CAMINO SIERRA

Henry Ford rolled his first Model T off the assembly line in September of 1908, and the culture of America's traveling public was forever changed. Henry Ford's "Tin Lizzie" was regarded as the first affordable automobile and provided inexpensive transportation to the growing middle class.

Americans across the land began taking advantage of their new-found mobility, traveling great distances for business and leisure. The only problem…the nation had very few decent roads to drive on, especially in the rural areas.

Motorists began clamoring for their governments to build new and better roads. Legislators were at first reluctant to allocate public funds for what might become a very expensive endeavor. "If the autoist wants new roads…let him pay for them himself," said California Governor James Gillett. In 1910, voters in the Golden State approved the State Highways Act authorizing $18-million in bonds for a "continuous and connected state highway system."

The lightly populated counties of Inyo and Mono knew they would have to go to extra lengths to obtain a share of the new highway funds. In Bishop, California, the Inyo Good Road Club formed with the purpose of obtaining better roads for the Eastern Sierra region. The primary mover behind this effort was the club's corresponding secretary, Wilfred G. Scott. Seeing the success coastal communities were enjoying in their efforts promoting a road through their area with the label El Camino Real, Scott devised a campaign to popularize the crude path through their counties as El Camino Sierra.

Over the next several years, Scott and the Inyo Good Road Club were relentless in their efforts to gain the attention of state legislators and highway engineers. Scott and the Club put on record setting plane flights, an auto tour covered by Sunset Magazine and even a local celebration that included the presence of Governor Gillett.

Thanks in large part to this tenacious promotion, the state did indeed begin to build and improve highways along El Camino Sierra. Each year several new highway projects were completed east of the Sierra Nevada.

Knowing he would need additional state monies to further improve his El Camino Sierra and other Eastern Sierra roads, Scott kept up his push to keep the state's focus on his area. Shortly after the entering of U.S. troops into World War I, Scott created the California National Defense Highway Association. Scott advocated that El Camino Sierra be designated a National Defense Military Road, whose purpose would be, "to constitute an inner line of defense along the east base of the Sierras, controlling all the mountain passes, extending northward along the Cascade Range to the Dalles, Oregon and into Washington, such as will insure the prosperity of the State, the security of the Republic and its preeminence in the family of nations."

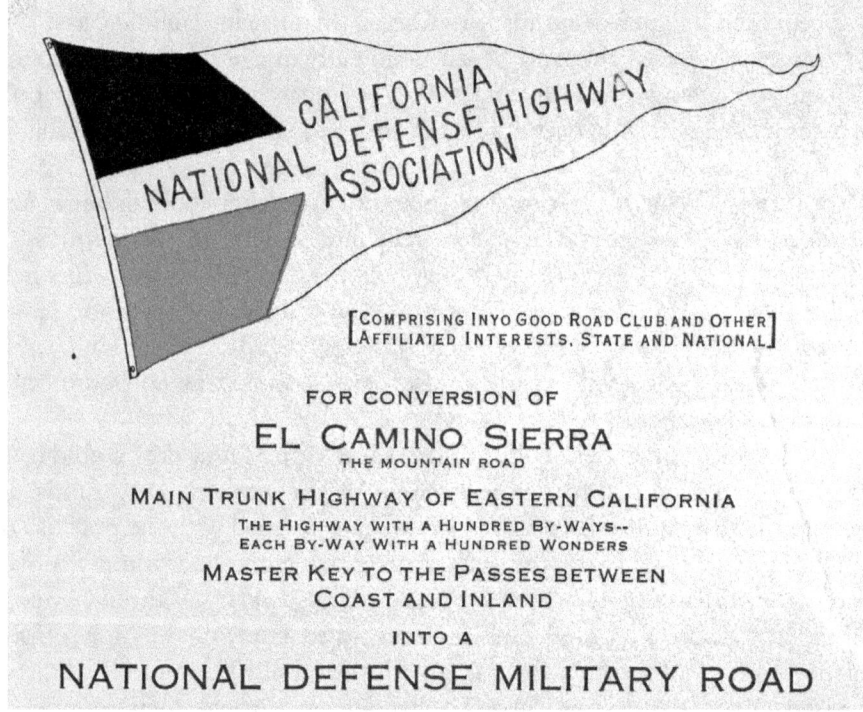

Figure 1-El Camino Sierra was promoted as an important link in our nation's defense during World War I

In March 1917, the state of Nevada created their own Department of Highways and improvements to roads throughout the Silver State were soon seen.

By 1931, a black topped or hard surfaced roadway had been completed the entire distance from Southern California to Lake Tahoe. Hundreds of thousands of travelers a year were using what the Los Angeles Times newspaper proclaimed, "one of the most beautiful scenic routes in the world."

Figure 2-The Inyo Good Road Club's El Camino Sierra would run from Mojave, California to Lake Tahoe

In 1934, the newly created Federal Bureau of Public Roads (now the Federal Highway Administration) declared that El Camino Sierra was to become part of a federal network of interstate roadways. The entire route was designated U.S. Highway 395 and extended from the Mexican border through California, Oregon and Washington to Canada.

Seeing the possibility for promoting the Eastern Sierra highway to an even bigger audience, the name El Camino Sierra was eventually set aside, and replaced by the new moniker, "Three Flags Highway" (Mexico, U.S. and Canada). Scott again took up the marketing and worked on promotional efforts with chamber of commerces from San Diego to Spokane.

But the Three Flags Highway never quite caught on. Scott passed away in 1937 and references to it are rarely seen after this time, though there are still a few businesses that incorporate "Three Flags" into their name.

For the past 80+ years, this magical roadway has been referred to as Highway 395 or more commonly…three-ninety-five. Whatever the name, perhaps nowhere else does a simple ribbon of blacktop have the ability to not only transport us to an such alluring spectacle as the sublime Eastern Sierra…but is also an avenue to a utopian state of mind.

| From
LOS ANGELES
To
RENO | | From
MEXICO
To
CANADA |

Figures 3, 4 & 5-El Camino Sierra was renamed the Three Flags Hwy for a short time starting in the 1930s, promoting its extension from Mexico to Canada

U.S.
Highway
395

Three
Flags
Highway

Mexico
to
Canada

Nevada
and
California
State Line
at
Topaz Lake

F-7551

CHAPTER TWO
FERRIS'S WHEEL

    Born in Illinois, five-year-old George Ferris Jr. came across the plains of the U.S. with his family who settled in Genoa, Nevada in 1859. Young Ferris was drawn to the Carson River and on hot summer afternoons, would climb on his pony and ride to the ribbon of refreshing coolness.

    Ferris's favorite spot was where the Carson River was spanned by the Cradlebaugh Bridge, a toll bridge that was part of the Overland Trail. The bridge was designed with an undershot waterwheel which scooped water out of the Carson River to irrigate farmer's crops in the nearby fields. It was said that Ferris would spend hours admiring and studying the simply designed apparatus.

    The Ferris family lived in the Carson Valley for two years before moving to nearby Carson City. George Ferris Sr. had an important impact on the development of Nevada's capital city. A former dairy farmer and expert in horticulture and agriculture, George Sr. played a large role in the beautification of Carson City in the 1870s. He landscaped the grounds of the Nevada State Capitol and brought trees native to the eastern part of the country to Nevada and planted them throughout Carson City.

    Upon graduation from high school, Ferris Jr. attended Rensselaer Polytechnic Institute in Troy, New York, earning a degree in engineering. He soon founded G.W.G. Ferris & Co, which specialized in assessing metals used in bridges and tunnels. George was very successful in his profession, but memories of that Carson River waterwheel never left him.

    In the years leading up to the 1893 Chicago World's Exposition, expo directors wanted to create an iconic attraction that would be unique and bring respect and grandeur to their event. Expo Manager Daniel Burnham argued that the Eiffel Tower, which was built by Gustave Eiffel just a few years earlier for the Paris Exposition of 1889, was leagues beyond anything American engineers had designed in recent memory. It was high time that the United States launched a cultural counter-punch to reclaim their prestige. Burnham invited engineers from across the U.S. to meet the challenge and design an attraction to impress the world.

Figure 6-Cradlebaugh Bridge on the Carson River about 1895

George Ferris Jr. heard of Burnham's challenge and reflected on that water wheel on the Caron River. Ferris drew out a simple design and after careful calculations, felt he had just the right creation. A massive 264-foot diameter suspended wheel with gondolas, that would carry up to 2,100 people at a time. George boasted that from the top vantage point, riders would be able to observe not only the entire Chicago area, but parts of Indiana and Wisconsin as well.

Burnham and the fair directors were impressed with Ferris's design and contracted with him to build his incredible "Ferris Wheel." Three thousand lights adorned the huge amusement ride on its inauguration, looking like a bright full moon during the evening hours. Ferris's wheel became the most popular attraction of the Chicago World's Expo.

Figure 7-Nevada's George Ferris Jr.'s Revolving Wheel at the Chicago Fair

The wheel had 36 cars, each fitted with 40 revolving chairs and able to accommodate up to 60 people, giving a total capacity of 2,160. The wheel carried up to 38,000 passengers daily and took 20 minutes to complete two revolutions, the first involving six stops to allow passengers to exit and enter and the second, a nine-minute non-stop rotation for which the ticket holder paid 50 cents. In less than five months, one and a half million people had taken a thrilling ride on Ferris's magnificent wheel.

After the Chicago World's Expo, the Ferris Wheel was dismantled and taken to the 1904 St. Louis Exposition, where it enjoyed another popular run. After the St. Louis Exposition, the wheel was returned to Chicago but left unassembled because it was just too expensive to keep it in operation. The wheel was eventually sold as scrap metal and was used to help build a large Navy ship, the U.S.S. Illinois during World War I.

George Ferris Jr. went back to his successful career as a civil engineer, but unfortunately contacted typhoid fever and soon passed away. But it was those lazy summer days spent beside the Carson River in Western Nevada, that provided Ferris's best idea, and found him a place of immortality in the culture of America.

Figure 8-George Ferris Jr. grew up in the Carson Valley and Carson City, Nevada where he spent many a dreamy afternoon on the banks of the Carson River, admiring and intrigued by a simple water wheel

CHAPTER THREE
BISHOP'S KITTIE LEE INN

There are many fine businesses that have made their mark along El Camino Sierra, and have since faded away into a distant fond memory. The Kittie Lee Inn in Bishop graced the northwest corner of Pine and Main Street for over 41 years and was at the forefront of the many fine hostelries that have offered welcoming accommodations to the weary Eastern Sierra traveler.

In 1923, local businessman Matt Wilkenson felt Bishop could easily support another high-end lodging option. The upscale Istalia Hotel, located on south Main Street, did a good business with the well heeled Bishop visitor, and Wilkenson saw an opportunity to enter the upscale hotel business himself.

Wilkenson purchased a lot on the northeast corner of Main and Pine streets and began construction. He opened his new hotel in the summer of 1924 and named it after his daughter, Kittie Lee. The fashionable Steps Orchestra was brought up from Los Angeles to play at the grand opening. The impressive structure was 151 feet long and 76 feet deep. It was built in classic California mission style with a red tile roof and a long shady front porch. Guests enjoyed a world class view of Mt. Tom from the porch's glider swings made of logs.

A massive fireplace occupied the hotel's east wall and is credited with being the salvation for many Bishop residents in 1933, when during a heavy snowstorm, the power went out and literally hundreds of local folks made their way to the Kittie Lee and crowded around the huge fireplace to not only stay warm, but to cook their meals as well.

Wilkenson sold his interest in the Kittie Lee just a year after it opened to William Whorff and Margaret McDonald. Whorff and McDonald worked hard and put their every effort into their investment, charging room rates accordingly. A double room with a private bath was a whopping $3.50 back in 1925.

Figure 9-The Kittie Lee Inn was as much a community gathering place as a place for overnight accommodations

It took most travelers two and a half days to make the trip along El Camino Sierra from Southern California to Bishop in the 1920s. The dusty, bumpy and sandy trip could try the patience of even the most seasoned motorist. But with the Kittie Lee Inn at the end of their long journey, travelers forged on knowing a relaxing time awaited them ahead. In short time, the alluring Kittie Lee became enormously popular and soon was considered "the" place to stay along El Camino Sierra.

During the 1920s and 30s, Hollywood filmed several movies in the Bishop area and movie stars found all the comforts of a big city hotel at the Kittie Lee. Guests to the hotel included Will Rogers, Hop Along Cassidy, Cary Grant, John Wayne, Kathryn Hepburn and Henry Fonda to name just a few. The Kittie Lee did such a large business with the film studios, Whorff and McDonald built a special dark room for the movie makers to keep their film in.

Whorff's son Bill recalled, "Many of those Hollywood stars were as friendly and unpretentious as could be. John Wayne was just an ordinary guy. He'd come into the coffee shop in the morning, sit at the counter and visit with people. He'd have his breakfast and never say who he was."

Brisk business continued at the Kittie Lee Inn up until World War II, when gas rationing quickly slowed tourist traffic to a near trickle. Fortunately, the military decided to use the Bishop airport as a training center for their pilots and the Army-Aircorp contracted with the owners of the Kittie Lee Inn to transform the Owens Valley landmark into a barracks for its soldiers stationed in Bishop. Demand for billeting the soldiers at the hotel became so great, the dining room was cleared out and dozens of cots brought in to house more soldiers. It's said that many a soldier fell in love with Bishop and the Owens Valley during their stay and returned frequently after the war had ended to enjoy the area's great outdoors.

Figure 10-The Kittie Lee featured comfortable elegance in a rustic setting

After the war, interest in traveling exploded and the Kittie Lee Inn was once again flush with visitors to the Eastern Sierra. The dining room was remodeled and became the Copper Kettle Coffee Shop. A small sleeping room attached to the Kittie Lee was converted into a cocktail lounge and was named Charlie's Bar after one of its regular local patrons.

The Kittie Lee operated into the 1960s, but progress eventually caught up with this Bishop institution and in 1965, it was torn down. All that remains of this legendary Bishop landmark is an historical plaque and beautiful mural depicting the Kittie Lee in all her glory, on the south side of Whiskey Creek Restaurant, which was built at the Kittie Lee's location.

Though their physical reminders may be gone…these fond memories we share from our collective past, will keep us comfortably grounded as we negotiate life's roadway…along El Camino Sierra.

Figure 11-the Kittie Lee Inn was a landmark in Bishop for over 40 years

Figure 12-The lobby of the Kittie Lee was a centerpiece of the historic hotel, featuring a huge fireplace and a piano where guests and locals would frequently gather to sing songs and enjoy each other's company

CHAPTER FOUR
A JEWEL OF TWO STATES

The beautiful gem of Topaz Lake glistens magically along the edge of El Camino Sierra as it traverses from California into Nevada, a few miles north of Coleville. The border between the two states passes almost directly through the center of the lake.

The freshwater reservoir impounds the west fork of the Walker River, one of the largest streams in the Eastern Sierra. The lake is extremely popular with anglers, boaters, skiers and campers, and also plays a large part in helping the Mason and Smith Valleys of Nevada be one of the most productive agricultural areas in the Silver State.

Farmers placed the fertile valley under cultivation as early as 1859, using water from the Walker River which flows through this area known as the Antelope Valley. The north end of the Antelope Valley was home to a small ephemeral pond named Alkali Lake. The pond was said to be brackish, and would dry up by the end of most summers.

In 1899, Nevada State senator and land baron Thomas Rickey, along with partner Reno banker Richard Kirman, already owned most of the water rights in the Antelope Valley including Alkali Lake, just over the state line in Nevada. The two planned to build a dam and transform the pond into a large reservoir by diverting the flow of the west fork of the Walker River into the sump and sell the water to Nevada ranchers and farmers.

Rickey had already firmly established himself in the ranching business in eastern California and western Nevada. He raised not only cattle, but sheep and horses. He owned over 42,000 acres in the Antelope Valley and Alpine County, as well as most of Long Valley which today is the site of Crowley Lake Reservoir in Mono County. He was one of the largest private landowners in the country at that time and his holdings made his the number one agri-business in the state of Nevada.

Litigation over who actually owned the Walker River water rights and panic in the financial markets tied up the project in courts and banks for the next 22 years. A court finally ruled in favor of the ranchers who had sued Rickey for unlawfully holding back downstream water. Due to his legal entanglements and the 1907 financial panic, Rickey's land holdings quickly eroded.

Figure 13-Topaz Lake has been an important stop on El Camino Sierra since just a few years after the road was built

In 1919, the lawsuit was finally settled by the U.S. Supreme Court and the Antelope Valley Land & Cattle Company took over the reservoir project. Money problems forced the Cattle Company to sell the reservoir site to farmers and ranchers in the Smith and Mason Valleys, who formed the Walker River Irrigation District (WRID).

WRID applied to the California State Water Commission and received permission to resume construction of the dam. Bond sales in 1921 funded the project which included a 2,100-foot tunnel to allow water to pass from the lake back into the West Walker River. The earthen dam was completed in 1922 and the reservoir began to fill. It held 45,000-acre feet when at full pool.

The irrigation district, thinking farmers may be hesitant to irrigate their lands from a body of water named Alkali, renamed their new jewel Topaz Lake. Very quickly, thousands of additional acres of Nevada land were placed under cultivation. With such increased demand, the WRID filed an application to build a levee which would nearly triple the reservoir's capacity to 126,00-acre feet. The levee was completed in 1937.

Figure 14-Fishing has always been popular at Topaz Lake

The surface area of the lake is approximately 2,410 acres and has been providing recreational opportunities to El Camino Sierra travelers since its completion. Because the lake is in both California and Nevada, a fishing license from either state is valid and Topaz Lake is actually at its best in the winter and early spring, when most bodies of water in the Eastern Sierra are frozen or buried under snow.

Over the years, birdwatching has also become a major form of recreation at the lake. Sightings include orioles, swallows, red-winged blackbirds and yellow warblers. The nest of a pair of bald eagles has been spotted near the Douglas County Park, while ospreys and pelicans are also frequently seen. During the spring and fall, the park's location on the primary migration route (Pacific Flyway) makes it an especially good bird-watching spot.

Being on the Nevada/California state line also made Topaz the perfect spot for a little gaming action. The historic Topaz Lake Lodge has been welcoming travelers to stop and rest…and try their luck since the early 1950s. Its colorful history includes ownership by both the Smith family of Harold's Club-Reno and Pick Hobson of the Riverside Hotel and Casino-Reno in years gone by. Today, the modern resort is a popular destination for travelers along El Camino Sierra and the center of activity for Topaz Lake recreation and entertainment.

Figure 15-Historic Topaz Lodge sits astride the Nevada/California border and has been the center of Topaz Lake recreation and entertainment since the 1950s

CHAPTER FIVE

DUNMOVIN

    Motorists traveling on El Camino Sierra about 14 miles south of Olancha, have probably noticed the ruins of a few dilapidated rock buildings with accompanying other small structures and mobile homes on the west side of the highway. This would be Dunmovin. A long existing real estate sign had announced the buildings and 170 acres of land with water rights for sale for a good number of years.

    Dunmovin came into existence around the end of the 19th century. It first served as a way station for the big freight wagons that hauled silver and supplies between the Cerro Gordo mining camp (high in the mountains southeast of Lone Pine) and Los Angeles. It was built by an early settler in the Owens Valley named James Cowan, who gave it the appropriate name of Cowan Station.

    Around 1908, while building their aqueduct, the Los Angeles Department of Water & Power (DWP) set up a construction camp nearby, due largely to the presence of five large springs above Cowan's, which provided a good supply of water for DWP's workers at the camp.

    Cowan eventually took on a partner by the name of Charles King. Wanting to retire to a more urban setting, Cowan sold the property to King and his wife Hilda in 1936. The Kings changed the name to Dunmovin. The story goes, that Hilda had tired of moving from town to town as her husband followed the mining opportunities of the west…and when they purchased the property from Cowan, she stated that she too… was "done moving." Wilson Olson in a little essay titled *Olancha Remembered* written in 1997, quotes a brief poem written by Hilda from the Olancha Journal circa 1940;

> *We've moved from yon to hither*
> *Now we're set and provin*
> *In all the world we are perhaps*
> *The only folks* **dunmovin**

Eventually there were other families living in the immediate area and in 1938, a post office operated at Dunmovin for a short period of time. The Kings put in a gas station, café, general store, and overnight accommodations, all of which were a welcoming site to travelers for several decades.

But as automobile travel became faster and more reliable…the need for stops like Dunmovin became less and less. Dunmovin closed its doors for good in in the early 1970s…but its many fond memories and tales it shares can still be recalled here…along El Camino Sierra.

Figure 16-Dunmovin was an important Eastern Sierra waystation up until the 1970s

CHAPTER SIX

FIRST IN FISHING

Trout fishing has been popular in the Eastern Sierra ever since the first rainbows were brought from the western slope and planted in Eastern Sierra streams during the 1870s. By the early 1900s, recreational anglers were enduring the bone jarring three-day trip from southern California on a rough and dusty El Camino Sierra to test their fishing skills, and in hopes of catching the "big one" in the Eastern Sierra.

Roy Carson from Pasadena was one of these early fishing pioneers. Roy loved fishing the lakes and streams of the June Lake area and couldn't believe his luck when he was able to obtain a year-round job working on the new Rush Creek power plant while on one of his fishing trips in 1916.

Figure 17-Happy anglers at Carson Camp-now Silver Lake Resort

Roy and his wife Nancy settled in and soon placed a few tents along the shores of Silver Lake, for their Pasadena friends to stay in when they would come up to visit and fish. The cluster of small tents became known as "Little Pasadena" since that was from whence most of Roy's friends hailed.

The Carsons would rent out the tents to other anglers when their friends weren't visiting. Over the next few years, they added permanent cabins and buildings and gave their property the official name of Carson Camp. It was the first recreational fishing camp in the Eastern Sierra.

Roy and Nancy worked tirelessly at providing an exceptional experience for their guests. Though the majority of the customers were fishermen, many people would come to stay at Silver Lake...simply to enjoy the incredible outdoor experience this magnificent area offered. Hollywood actor Wallace Beery was so taken in with the area's scenic beauty, he built a vacation cabin not far from Carson Camp.

Carson Camp was eventually renamed Silver Lake Resort. The Carsons sold their gem in 1941, and the resort has changed hands only twice since. In a testament to this magic property's appeal, the current owners have operated Silver Lake for over 40 years and continue with its long history of providing warm hospitality and exceptional customer service.

Next time you're in the area, stop in at Silver Lake Resort to enjoy and appreciate a genuine piece of Eastern Sierra history and hospitality at its finest. Look at the many photos taken over the years of the thousands of happy anglers and vacationers you'll see posted on the wall...and ponder for a moment the wonderful life experiences and lasting memories this legendary property has created for over a hundred years now.

Figure 18-Silver Lake Resort has been creating special memories for over 100 years

CHAPTER SEVEN
A NATURAL SCENE

    Anne Brigman was an artistic photographer and one of the original members of the Photo-Secession movement in America. Photo-Secessionists championed the idea that a photograph need not be slavishly dedicated to the depiction of reality, but instead, composed and even manipulated to deliver a compelling subjective vision. Brigman is perhaps best known for her work during the early 1900s, that depict nude women in primordial, naturalistic contexts.

    Brigman was born in Hawaii in 1869. She was briefly married to a sea captain before divorcing and moving to the San Francisco Bay area, where she embraced the growing bohemian movement. While there, she also became friends with writer Jack London and poet Charles Keeler.

    Seeking her own artistic outlet, Brigman began photographing in 1901, and soon developed a reputation as a master of pictorial photography. Her photographs became collector items and she opened a teaching studio in Berkeley. Her celebrity status was confirmed in 1907 when the San Francisco Call featured Brigman and her works in a full-page Sunday magazine article.

    Galleries in New York, Washington D.C. and even London, England were exhibiting her work. As her popularity continued to grow, Brigman offered revealing insight into the liberation of women in a male dominated society.

    So, what does Bay area photographer Anne Brigman have to do with the Eastern Sierra? Brigman's photographs frequently focused on the female nude, dramatically situated in natural landscapes or trees. Many of her nude photos were taken in the wilds of the Sierra Nevada and Eastern California, in carefully selected locations and featuring elaborately staged poses.

    Brigman often featured herself as the subject of her nude artistic images, such as her famous *Soul of the Blasted Pine* (1909) which was taken during a solo trip Brigman made into the remote Bristlecone Pine forest of the

White Mountains. In fact, most of Brigman's photography trips into the wilds of Eastern California were made alone.

Figure 19-Anne Brigman was characterized by a free-spirited nature

She would hike and pack into the mountains with enough provisions to allow her to work for two weeks to two months. She would photograph her topics, typically in the nude and in these pure settings, make them integral to it. Her preparation for the scene was meticulous, removing unattractive stones and pebbles, making the method as necessary as the ultimate outcome.

Figure 20-The wilds of the Sierra Nevada Mountains were one of Brigman's favorite locations to work

Brigman's counter-cultural images suggested bohemianism and female liberation. Her work challenged the establishment's cultural norms and defied convention. The raw emotional intensity and barbaric strength of her photos contrasted with the carefully calculated and composed images of other modern photographers of her time.

Figure 21-Brigman's work often hinted at Greco-Roman mythology

Brigman moved south to Long Beach, California in 1929 to be near her family and it was here that her artistic style began to change. Brigman expanded her creative output to include drawings, prints, etchings and poetry. She created mock-ups for three books combining her own poems with photographs, one of which was published--*Songs of the Pagan*-(1949).

Not only was Anne Brigman a pioneer in artistic photography, she helped pave the way for an entire generation and beyond of women…to have confidence in themselves to go out on their own and pursue their life passion and interests.

Figure 22-Anne Brigman self-portrait-Yosemite

CHAPTER EIGHT

FALES HOT SPRINGS

Fales Hot Springs is another legendary landmark that has woven itself tightly into our nostalgic memories of Eastern Sierra history. For over 150 years, many an El Camino Sierra traveler has enjoyed the welcoming charm and hospitality of this northern Mono County institution.

In the late 1850s, the Eastern Sierra was awash with promising ore strikes at Monoville, Dogtown, Aurora and Bodie. Prospectors were crossing the mountains from Sonora using an old Native American trail, passable only to foot and horse traffic. An improved route that could handle wagon traffic would be needed to accommodate the influx of gold seekers.

Community members and government officials from Mono, San Joaquin, Stanislaus and Tuolumne Counties met in 1863, for the purpose of arranging the financing of a Sonora-Mono Wagon Road. $400,000 and five years later, a crude road between Sonora on the west slope and Bridgeport on the east was completed.

Hoping to take advantage of the influx of traffic expected on the new Sonora-Mono wagon road, Samuel Fales purchased a natural hot spring along the route just a few miles north of the geologic feature known as Devils Gate. Sam and his brother Tom worked hard on the property and developed it into a fully operational hotel and bathhouse known as the Hot Springs Hotel.

An article in the Bridgeport Chronicle-Union praised the curative waters of the springs and noted the dinner table at the hotel was supplied with the "luxuries of the season."

Competing waystations were opened nearby. Hiram Leavitt built a roadhouse at Leavitt Meadows, the first encountered after descending Sonora Pass. Frank Pickel operated a hotel and trading post a few miles to the east of Leavitt. The nearby meadows were later named for him.

Leavitt eventually moved to Bridgeport where he opened a new hotel and stage stop, which is now the Bridgeport Inn. Leavitt became a prominent local citizen and served as a Mono County judge.

Figure 23-Samuel Fales

The hot springs reached its peak in the 1890s. In addition to offering dinner and a dip in the rejuvenating hot water for 50 cents, the hotel featured live music and dancing late into the evening. Sam's resort gradually came to be known as Fales Hot Springs.

Looking to "scale back" a bit as he entered his golden years, Sam Fales leased his resort to J.M. Mawer in 1908. Sam continued to live at the hot springs, entertaining the guests with his many tall tales. Mawer renovated the baths and made several improvements. An advertisement from 1910 states "careful and competent attendants were standing by to assist patrons."

In the 1920s, Bridgeport brothers Slick & Merrick Bryant installed a ski run three miles south of Fales Hot Springs near Devils Gate. The modest ski area operated until the outbreak of World War II. Nearby Fales Resort offered meals, lodging and a warm soak for the adventurous winter enthusiasts.

When Sam Fales died in 1933 at 104 years of age, his heirs first leased the property to a variety of hoteliers and then sold it outright. A 1940 edition of the Bridgeport Chronicle-Union proclaimed that Fales Hot Springs was the place to "dine, dance and romance." Cabins with bath were $2.00 nightly. Special Sunday dinners included rabbit or baked Virginia ham for $1.00. At the 1940 Christmas Eve party, each guest was given a Christmas tree, gifts and a dinner buffet, all for $2.50

New owners installed a Richfield gas station up near the highway in the mid-1940s, but a propane explosion burnt Fales to the ground in 1952. The owners rebuilt the resort with a new restaurant, lounge and pool. The new and improved Fales enjoyed a steady business. A 1955 edition of the Bridgeport newspaper even reported that "a group had gathered in the lounge at Fales to watch the Academy Awards presentation on television."

New Cafe and Cocktail Lounge

* MINERAL TUB BATHS . . . SWIMMING POOL
* HOUSEKEEPING CABINS
* SERVICE STATION . . . STORE

On U. S. Highway 395 . . . 14 miles north of Bridgeport, in Mono County, Calif. Elev. 7,300

Fales Hot Springs

Post Office:
BRIDGEPORT, CALIF.   Telephone: BRIDGEPORT 8515

Figure 24-A brochure from the 1950s

Over the next 40 years, Fales Hot Springs went through a number of different owners…with many big dreams. But as cars became more fuel efficient and travelers were encouraged to continue further north to Lake Tahoe and Reno, business at Fales declined. Eventually, the weary cabins were torn down along with the filling station. The last of Fales Hot Springs Resort closed in 1990.

Figure 25 & 26 (above & below)-Fales Hot Springs in the early 1930s

A fair amount of work has been done at Fales in recent years, and reports are that the current owners hope to reopen the hotel and hot springs to the public again someday. But for now, it is closed to the public…and our enjoyment of Fales will have to be confined to the many warming memories we enjoy of this historic Eastern Sierra landmark.

CHAPTER NINE

THE RIGHT THING

Thousands of Americans voiced their concern over the unjust treatment of the 110,000 Japanese-American citizens and immigrants, who were forced into internment camps by the U.S. Government at the start of World War II. Many organizations from churches to civil rights groups vigorously denounced the government's actions. There were also thousands of individuals who took it upon themselves to do what they felt was right, in defense of those that were interned.

Born in Los Angeles in 1924, Ralph Lazo was of Mexican-Irish descent and grew up in the Temple-Beaudry area of Los Angeles. The neighborhood was integrated and included families of Caucasian, Jewish, Japanese, Filipino, Korean, Mexican and Chinese descent. Ralph was a popular student at Belmont High School and was active in sports and in student government.

After the Empire of Japan attacked Pearl Harbor on December 7, 1941, Japanese-Americans increasingly became targeted as disloyal Americans. On February 19, 1942, President Franklin D. Roosevelt signed Executive Order 9066, which required 110,000 persons of Japanese ancestry, two-thirds of whom were U.S. citizens, report to temporary "assembly centers" and later transferred to ten internment camps located in the country's interior.

Ralph Lazo watched anxiously as his Japanese-American neighbors hurriedly sold their personal belongings (including homes and businesses) and registered their families for confinement in the internment camps.

Yoshindo Shibuya was Ralph's classmate and friend at Belmont High School. After Yoshindo was sent to Manzanar, he wrote to Ralph and a few weeks later, received a letter in return. Ralph told Yoshindo to expect him to arrive at Manzanar on a certain date. To Yoshindo's surprise, Ralph arrived at camp with some of his Japanese-American high school friends and their families on the date promised, having taken the train from Los Angeles to Lone Pine and then a bus to Manzanar.

Figure 27-17 year old Ralph Lazo was the only person known to have "voluntarily" join his Japanese-American friends inside an internment camp

Even as a young seventeen-year-old, Ralph felt the internment of Japanese-Americans was unjust. He had learned the U.S. Constitution in school and thought forcing his friends and neighbors into these camps violated their civil rights in every way. In the truest measure of standing up for what one believes in, Ralph voluntarily placed himself behind the barbed wire of Manzanar to stand resolute with his friends.

"Internment was immoral," Lazo told the *Los Angeles Times*. "It was wrong, and I couldn't accept it. These people hadn't done anything that I hadn't done except to go to Japanese language school. I had to go with them to show my support."

After Ralph's family learned that he was at the internment camp and not at "summer camp," Ralph's sister Virginia wrote several letters asking Ralph to return home. But Ralph did not want to return and his father eventually gave him permission to stay at Manzanar. Ralph became an active member of the Manzanar community, playing sports and being elected president of his class at Manzanar High School.

Figure 28-Ralph and his teammates on the Manzanar High School baseball team. Ralph is in the dark striped t-shirt, lower left

Following graduation from Manzanar High School, Ralph was drafted into the armed services and served in the Pacific Theater, where he made rank of staff sergeant and was awarded the Bronze Star for heroism in combat.

After the war, Ralph returned to Los Angeles, earning a master's degree from Cal State Northridge. He spent his career teaching, mentoring disabled students and encouraging minorities to attend college and vote. Ralph also worked on the Civil Liberties Act of 1988, which offered an official apology and reparations to Japanese American interned during World War II, from the U.S. government.

Ralph Lazo stayed in touch with his Japanese-American friends for his entire life. The bonds he made with them were eternal and he never forgot the unjust way they were treated.

Figure 29-Ralph Lazo (right) remained life-long friends with many of the Japanese-Americans he joined in internment at Manzanar

On New Year's Day 1992, one of Ralph's Japanese-American friends came by Ralph's home to drop off some of his favorite Japanese New Year's dishes. It was then she learned from his family of his recent passing.

With Ralph's death, Japanese Americans lost a dear friend and the world lost a great man of unflinching conviction and integrity. When it seemed the whole world was against a single culture of people, Ralph Lazo stood by them, kept their spirits up and refused to turn his back on them.

CHAPTER TEN

RENO'S FIRST DESTINATION

Long before the arrival of the resort casinos, Reno, Nevada had a world class destination resort that rivaled those found in America's largest cities. A few miles southwest of downtown Reno lies an area of warm water springs. Evidence suggests these springs have been enjoyed by Native Americans long before the arrival of euro-settlers.

By the beginning of the 20th century, many Reno residents were familiar with the warm pools located on what was then the Haines Ranch. In the summer of 1905, Charles T. Short, Al North and John N. Evans purchased the ranch with plans for developing a resort. Short had lived in the Hawaiian Islands for a time and had stayed at a resort by the name of Moana Springs. He convinced North and Evans it was the right name for their new project.

The investors first hired well drillers, who quickly brought forth a significantly increased quantity of warm water. Work soon began on building a large bath house, swimming pool and six small rooms with private hot pools. A second phase would bring a clubhouse, a fifty-room hotel and dining room.

Construction began in August of 1905 and by October, the swimming pool and hot pools were open to the public. Perhaps because it was fall and the cooler weather of northern Nevada was setting it, the large indoor naturally heated pool was an immediate success. Entrepreneurs offered auto and carriage service from downtown Reno out to Moana. The hotel was completed the next year and Moana Baths became northern Nevada's premiere destination resort.

Many of its guests believed the warm mineral water provided relief for a number of ailments and word spread of Moana's curative powers. Its water was bottled and sold throughout northern Nevada and California. Many out of towners who had come to Reno to wait out the required six months to get a divorce, would idle away their time soaking in the warm waters.

Figure 30-Moana Springs was Reno's first destination resort

Business continued to grow and by October of 1907, the Nevada Interurban Railway, a trolley line owned by Louis W. Berrum, began service to Moana Springs from downtown Reno.

Figure 31-Reno's streetcar line was extended to Moana Springs due to its popularity. Here a streetcar can be seen crossing the Truckee River heading south

Enjoying their success and looking for other means to grow and expand the business at their popular resort, the owners started work on excavating a large lake for winter ice skating and summer boating.

Short, North and Evans brought in other shareholders, including the Interurban's Berrum, who also owned adjoining property to Moana. But apparently success created friction among the investors, and the resort actually closed for a period in 1911 while legal problems were litigated.

Berrum came out on top and took sole control over Moana Springs after settling with the other investors. The Berrum family operated Moana for the next forty-three years. Additional improvements brought on by Berrum included a popular dance hall, a motion picture theater, an ice skating and boating lake and a baseball diamond. Berrum even planted an orchard surrounding the resort, giving the entire property an estate feel.

In 1912, Moana Springs' manager Jack Steele brought in aviators Frank Bryant and Roy Francis to stage one of Reno's earliest aerial exhibitions. The event must have been popular as other aerialists, hot air balloonists and even parachutists performed there over the next several years.

For most of the nineteen-teens and twenties, Moana Springs was "the place" in the Reno area. School parties, weddings, big top circuses, and shooting demonstrations were routinely held at Moana's extensive grounds. Berrum would bring rodeos to the property to support Reno's association with the old west.

Boxing matches were another popular venue held at Moana. In the summer of 1910, ex-heavyweight champion Jim Jeffries trained at Moana Springs for his comeback "Fight of the Century" against Jack Johnson. A few years later, Jess Willard fought a match at Moana on his ascension to the heavyweight title.

Baseball may have been the historic property's biggest claim to fame. Exhibition games were held at a simple ballfield on the site from the days the resort first opened. An official ballpark was built in 1946 with the Reno Silver Sox of the old Sunset League moving there in 1947. That original Moana Stadium burned down in 1956, with a replacement facility opening the following season as the home of the Reno Silver Sox of the

Figure 32-Former heavyweight champ Jim Jeffries trained at Moana for his Reno fight

California League. Affiliated ball was played there off and on until 1992. It also hosted independent ball from 1996-1999.

Figure 33-Moana Field was home to various Reno baseball teams for almost 70 years

Louis Berrum passed away in 1940, but his wife and son kept the property going on into the 1950s. The City of Reno purchased the Moana property in 1956 and everything but the ballpark was demolished in December of 1957 to make way for a modern sports complex.

Today, the city of Reno operates the area as Moana Springs Recreation Complex. As of spring of 2019, there are plans afoot by the Reno community to construct a new public pool, using the warm waters that have been the mainstay of this historic western Nevada gem.

CHAPTER ELEVEN

KING OF THE JUNGLE

The construction of the Los Angeles Aqueduct is arguably one of the most significant events that have happened in modern times. The colossal engineering and construction project spawned a litany of new methods and concepts from transportation to health care.

When construction was about to begin on this huge public works project in 1908, Superintendent William Mulholland knew he would need an extensive medical program for the thousands of workers and laborers that would be employed in the dangerous construction work.

Mulholland called upon Dr. Raymond Taylor, who was president of the Los Angeles Medical Association at that time, to head up the aqueduct's new health care program. A contract was signed with the Water Department in May of 1908 and Taylor hit the ground running to get the huge effort underway.

At its peak, over 6,000 workers would be stationed at several construction camps along the aqueducts 233-mile route. Taylor would provide field hospitals and emergency medical stations to care for the sick and injured along the entire distance of the construction project. Finding enough qualified medical staff to work in such remote and isolated locations would not be easy. The work was as demanding on hospital stewards and medical staff as on the construction workers themselves.

At one specific point in time, Dr. Taylor was hard pressed to fill a hospital steward position. One of the applicants was a husky, 6-foot, 230-pound young man by the name of Otto Elmo Linkenheldt. Linkenheldt claimed to have had some experience in first aid and Dr. Taylor thought he seemed intelligent enough and willing to work. Dr. Taylor hired Linkenheldt and sent him out to one of the aqueduct's field hospitals. By all accounts, Link (as Dr. Taylor called him) did a good job caring for the workers in the remote and isolated Owens Valley, where he worked until the completion of the aqueduct in 1913.

Figure 34-The 6,000 workers who helped build the LA Aqueduct kept the medical services of Dr. Taylor and his staff busy

After he returned to Los Angeles, Linkenheldt stopped in to see Dr. Taylor one day, saying he had a job with one of the motion picture companies as a first-aid man and an extra on location near Chatsworth, where D. W. Griffith was making a "primitive man" picture. Griffith thought it likely they might experience an accident or two as they were working on a steep rock cliff.

Linkenheldt asked if he could have one of the first-aid kits he had used while working on the aqueduct in the Owens Valley. The doctor agreed and fixed him up with a few other items he thought Link might need.

After the filming was completed at Chatsworth, the movie company decided to go to the swamps of Louisiana, where the long-limbed, overhanging trees made an ideal location to produce jungle scenes for the first Tarzan film, "*Tarzan of the Apes*." Griffith asked Linkenheldt if he would accompany them again as a first-aid man and extra. Link agreed.

On location in Louisiana, the Tarzan actor from New York was a bit moody. He refused to wade around in the swamp, swing from tree to tree, or dodge an occasional water moccasin. He soon reached the end of his proverbial rope…and quit. The departure of the leading man left the company stuck in the swamp without a Tarzan.

Link had been watching the filming for several weeks and felt he could fill the role. Being muscular, athletic and active, Link told Griffith he could be his Tarzan. Griffith let him do a few scenes, was impressed, and hired Link to do the whole picture. Griffith then gave Link the stage name of Elmo Lincoln, and the rest as they say, is movie history.

Figure 35-Linkenheldt (Lincoln) worked in over sixty films

Lincoln played the role of Tarzan in two more movies, *The Romance of Tarzan* and The *Adventures of Tarzan*, the last being in 1920. He also appeared in several other movies during the late nineteen-teens.

Dr. Taylor recalled how his friend Link stopped by his office one day, shortly after filming his last Tarzan movie. As the doctor recalled, Lincoln was "all scarred up," so he asked him what had happened. "Well," Lincoln said, "I was wrestling with a lion the other day and the old fool got rough and scratched me up." The doctor said, "Oh, do you do that often?" "Oh, yes." Lincoln replied. "We've got a couple of tame old beasts anybody can fool with. They haven't got any teeth, but they've got claws. I wasn't quick enough, and I got messed up." Lincoln actually had killed the lion with a knife during the attack.

After 1920, Lincoln's movie career declined from the height of his Tarzan days. The introduction of sound in motion pictures didn't work well for Link. He left Hollywood and moved to Salt Lake City, where he operated a salvage business for a number of years, before returning to Hollywood in 1937 to work again in films.

Lincoln worked in over sixty films, including *Birth of a Nation* and *The Kaiser*, but most of his appearances were as an extra or stand-in. His last films were *Joan of Arc* and *The Hollywood Story*, in which he played himself. Tarzan of the LA aqueduct died in Los Angeles on June 27, 1952 at the age of sixty-three. His very full career having got its start…along El Camino Sierra.

Figure 36-Three Tarzan movies featured Lincoln as the "King of the Jungle"

CHAPTER TWELVE
TUFA REFRIGERATOR OF MONO LAKE

Most everyone is familiar with the unusual rock formations at Mono Lake known as tufa towers. The tufa is essentially common limestone. What is uncommon about this limestone is the way it forms. Underwater springs at Mono Lake that are rich in calcium, mix with lake water which is heavy with carbonates. As the calcium comes in contact with carbonates in the lake, a chemical reaction occurs resulting in calcium carbonate-or limestone. The calcium carbonate settles out of solution as a solid around the spring, and over the course of decades to centuries, a tufa tower will develop. Tufa towers grow exclusively underwater, and some grow to a height of 30 feet. When the lake level recedes due to diversions or drought, the tufa becomes exposed above the lake level, often on dry land.

Close to the lake's west shore, is one of the many clusters of tufa at Mono Lake. On an area that was once known as the Nay Ranch, is a fairly large tufa formation, about 15' high, with a natural hollow or cave opening inside the tufa.

Mono Basin pioneer family member Lily La Braque remembers living on the Nay Ranch as a youngster. In Lily's book, *Man from Mono*, she recalls an ice-cold spring gurgling up from the ground inside the tufa cave. Lily says the cave became their refrigerator. It had a hole in the top for ventilation, and a natural shelf where the La Braque's stored eggs, butter and milk. Lily also said they would occasionally hang mutton and beef inside the natural refrigerator.

Several years ago, we located the La Braque's tufa refrigerator. There was no spring at the time, but the inside of the tufa was indeed twenty-five degrees or more, cooler that in the warm July sun outside.

The La Braque's sold their ranch after the great 1906 San Francisco earthquake. Lily recounted for several weeks after the quake, Mono Lake's level rose 30 feet or more, inundating pastures, fences and eventually the ground floor of their house, making life along the shore of ancient Mono Lake, impossible.

Figure 37-The Tufa Refrigerator of Mono Lake

We always urge folks to make time to explore the many secret treasures of the Eastern Sierra. If you have the time, see if you can find the Tufa Refrigerator of Mono Lake and enjoy the "cool" history that this old natural formation has created.

CHAPTER THIRTEEN

JAILHOUSE TREASURE

In 1885, the prosperous mining town of Virginia City, Nevada was still producing gold and silver. A stage coach from the famous Wells Fargo company was tasked with getting a $62,000 deposit of gold from Virginia City to the U.S. Mint in Carson City, fifteen miles away.

The stage was driven by one William Manners with guard Mike O'Fallon keeping an eye out for any trouble. There were also passengers inside the coach headed to the state capital.

Part way through the trip, Manners stopped at the settlement of Empire to give the passengers a chance to get out of the dusty stage to take a brief break, and to water the horses. Manners hurried the group along and soon resumed the trip.

As the stage with its precious cargo neared the outskirts of Carson City, four holdup artists with guns drawn halted the stage. With Manner's and O'Fallon's hands in the air, the bad guys removed the strong box of gold and demanded the passengers give them all their valuables as well. They took their loot and left the frightened travelers and helpless Wells Fargo men high and dry in the desert.

Manners speeded the coach in to town and alerted the sheriff. A posse was quickly gathered, and the group struck out to find the desperados. The outlaws were found in short order and a gun battle ensued. Dozens of shots were fired and three of the bandits were killed. The fourth, the notorious Manuel Gonzalez was taken into custody. Luckily, not a single member of the posse was even wounded.

Despite the quick capture, the strong box of gold and the passenger's belongings were nowhere to be found. Gonzalez was interrogated for days by the lawmen, but he never said a word. Gonzalez was sentenced to twenty years confinement in the Nevada State Prison in Carson City for his part in the robbery.

Gonzalez is said to have bragged to fellow prisoners, and even prison guards, that he could see where the gold and jewelry was buried from the window of his cell. He was paroled after only eight years for good behavior, but mysteriously, Gonzalez died of "natural causes" just a few weeks after gaining his freedom.

Prison guards purportedly searched for the missing treasure in their off time, using the view from Gonzalez's cell as their sight. The prison was closed in 2012 and as far as is known, the gold and jewelry has still never been found. But then again…who would say if they did?

Figure 38 & 38A-The Nevada State Prison in Carson City

CHAPTER FOURTEEN
A WOMAN TO MATCH THE MOUNTAINS

Nellie Bly Baker is one of the most interesting people to have ever called the land along El Camino Sierra home. College educated, secretary, motion picture camera person, Hollywood movie star, fishing guide and resort operator… are just a few of the many faces of Sierra legend Nellie Bly.

Nellie was born in Oklahoma in 1893. Even from her early years, she showed an adventuresome and fearless spirit. Everything in nature interested Nellie, and she seemed to have a natural ability to handle wild animals of all kind. She loved the outdoors and as a young lady, her older brothers taught her how to ride, fish and handle firearms. This outdoor way of life prepared Nellie for what would become an unconventional lifestyle many years later.

In hopes it might tame her wild spirit, Nellie's parents sent her to a convent for two years. Convent life didn't seem to slow her down much, but it did teach her the value of graceful manners and the benefits of a good education.

Nellie completed two years of college at Texas A&M, got married, got divorced, moved to Hollywood and soon became the PBX operator in Charlie Chaplain's office. Chaplain recognized Nellie's natural talent and her beauty was quite evident. Chaplain cast her in her first movie in 1923, in which critics showered praise upon this previously unknown beauty.

Nellie's movie career took off. In the next 20 years, she had roles in 48 motion pictures. She appeared in films with such stars as Greta Garbo, Joan Crawford and Clark Gable.

Nellie wanted a guesthouse and pool built on her Hollywood Hills property. Though her income was substantial, Nellie felt the contractors quote for their construction work was too high, so she decided she would build the pool and guesthouse herself. In what spare time she could find in her busy schedule, Nellie diligently taught herself the necessary skills, and completed both projects within a year. She now could add carpenter and mason to her long list of abilities.

Figure 39-Nellie got her Hollywood start with Charlie Chaplin

In the early 1930s, Nellie was on location in Mammoth Lakes filming the movie *Thundering Herd*. Nellie was awe struck with the beauty of the Eastern Sierra. She returned the next year to spend a summer vacation hunting and fishing and decided this was the place she had to be.

The pull of the mountains was strong and by 1938, Nellie purchased property in Lundy Canyon near Mono Lake. Dreaming of a life in the mountains instead of on a Hollywood movie set, Nellie began work on building a small resort she named Happy Landing. Nellie used the lumber from the old mining cabins that had been abandoned in Lundy Canyon to build her resort. Using the carpentry skills she had developed while building the pool and guesthouse at her Hollywood home, she built a residence for herself, several smaller cabins and a store and café. Nellie painted murals on the various building walls at Happy Landing and spread her art to nearby boulders. The famous Indian Chief along the road near the Lundy Canyon beaver ponds is a Nellie work still enjoyed today.

With no electricians in the Mono Basin at that time, Nellie studied, and took the test to become a licensed electrician so she could work on her own wind and diesel driven power sources.

Nellie's first winter brought the deepest snows of her thirteen winters at Lundy Canyon. She later recounted she used a full-length mink coat from her Hollywood days, as an expensive but very functional nightshirt.

Avalanches were commonplace, and a falling rock once came so close to her cabin she deemed the fact that she had survived it, an act of God.

Her first full summer was a busy one. She cooked breakfast, lunch and dinner for her guests, cleaned cabins and guided many of the fishermen and hunters into the backcountry. She became the first woman in the state of California to hold a license as a fishing and hunting guide. Nellie Bly Baker became the queen of Eastern Sierra hospitality. Her popularity was so impassioned, that many of her clients found a way to make it to Nellie's even during the gas rationing days of World War II.

Figure 40-Nellie Bly guided thousands of outdoorsmen/women into the Sierra backcountry and was the first licensed female hunting/fishing guide in the state

In 1952, as Nellie was approaching her 60th birthday, she made the decision to make more time for herself and sold Happy Landing Resort. But Nellie stayed on in her beloved Eastern Sierra. She leased property near Mono Lake from Wally MacPherson, the owner of the nearby Mono Inn, and began a life of what she thought would be rest and relaxation…but she soon found otherwise.

Years before, while leading a pack trip from Lundy Canyon, Nellie came upon a miner's cabin that had tumbled down into a canyon from a cliff high above. The cabin had landed intact, but upside down, with many of the furnishings neatly arranged in the new odd position.

The experience had brought back memories to Nellie from her childhood, where she had loved the children's story of the two sisters who sailed to the "land of upside down." Nellie knew the story by heart…and in time, another facet of her remarkable life took place when she was able to build a replica of the topsy-turvy cabin.

Nellie brought in lumber and hauled tables, chairs and a stove as well as other household goods to her site. Nellie began construction of her upside-down house, replete with a thermometer on an outside wall, that of course, was upside down. When completed, thousands of tourists found their way to Nellie's Upside-down House. It was considered one of the major tourist attractions in all of Mono County. In retirement, Nellie also continued to lead guided pack trips into the backcountry. At age 71, she led her last trip, a party of 10 over 10,000' passes and hiking 10 miles in. She helped form the Mono County Chamber of Commerce, contributed a weekly column to the Bridgeport newspaper and wrote several articles about her life and the many characters she had met during her time in the mountains.

Figure 41-Nellie Bly in front of her famous Upside-Down House of the Mono Basin

Nellie spent her final years at a rest home in Lone Pine, passing away peacefully at age 91. Her upside-down house was eventually moved to the town of Lee Vining where it can be viewed today, next to the Mono Basin Historical Society's Museum. Pioneering Eastern Sierran Nellie Bly always forged her own way and whose legacy will stand forever…along El Camino Sierra.

CHAPTER FIFTEEN
MINDEN HERITAGE

The Douglas County town of Minden, Nevada is proud of its history and heritage. Founded in 1905 by Carson Valley pioneer H.F. Dangberg, Jr., the town would become the hub for the valley's agrarian based economy. Dangberg thought he could convince the Virginia and Truckee (V&T) Railroad that it would be profitable for it to extend a spur line from Carson City to the new town, to haul the farmer's crops. With ready access to larger markets, more farmers would come to the Carson Valley and the new town would flourish.

Figure 42-The Minden Flour Mill is a perfect example of high quality craftmanship

Central to Minden's agricultural base was the growing of wheat. The first of five flour mills in the Carson Valley was built in 1854, to provide the staple to the growing influx of miners to the area. The last mill built was the Minden Flour Milling Company and it continues today to sit proudly in central Minden as an important reminder of the town's rich history.

Figure 43-Agriculture has long been a mainstay of the Carson Valley economy

The architectural style of the Mill reflects the transition from the more remote "country mills" built by the local ranchers, to the larger mills constructed by the railroad companies beside their tracks for mass distribution of mill products to other areas. The craftsmanship in the Minden building is one of few remaining examples displaying the traditional high quality of northern European and early American carpentry and masonry. This type of workmanship is rare to nonexistent in later construction found throughout the west.

The mill consists of two sections: a three-story brick mill building with a gable roof and stepped parapet gable end walls, and a cluster of four 45-foot-high steel silos covered by a sheet-metal gable roof. One-story additions on the south and east sides of the brick structure were completed in 1908. The bricks for the massive structure were fired in a kiln built directly next to the mill.

Local farmers made good use of the mill from the start and it was also a principal reason the power company decided to extend electric transmission to the Carson Valley, which not only provided electricity for the mill, but for the good citizens of Minden and Gardnerville as well.

By the 1920s, the mill had become one of the biggest milling concerns in the state producing 100 barrels of flour a day. In later years, the mill also produced chicken and cattle feed. The mill reliably served the farmers and ranchers of the Carson Valley until the 1960s.

The Minden Flour Milling Company building is located in a unique complex of other Minden historical sites. Approximately 125 feet to the north of the mill is the handsome one-story brick Minden Butter

Manufacturing Company building built in 1916. This historic creamery was designed by Frederic J. DeLongchamps, one of Nevada's most celebrated commercial architects. It was the largest creamery in Nevada at its peak. The building was added to the National Register of Historic Places on August 6, 1986.

Figure 44-The Minden Flour Mill was one of the largest producing mills in the state

Figure 45-The construction of the Minden Flour Mill played an important role in convincing the V&T Railroad to build a spur line to Minden

Today, this complex of historic buildings has taken on a new life thanks to Bently Heritage, LLC. The Carson Valley based company has breathed new life into the historic structures, extensively remodeling, renovating and reconstructing the beautiful buildings into a world class distillery of fine spirits. Today, visitors can delight in a tour of the distillery, reminisce in its history and enjoy a visit to the tasting room.

Figure 46-The Minden Butter Company building is part of a complex of historic structures in Minden

Figure 47-Local Carson Valley company Bently Heritage LLC has transformed the flour mill and creamery into a world class distillery of fine spirits

CHAPTER SIXTEEN

LONE PINE OBSERVATORY

Mt. Whitney has been a popular attraction ever since it was determined to be the highest peak in the lower 48 states. Climbers, explorers and every day adventurers were soon making their way towards its lofty summit.

In the 1920s, William Probasco was a highly regarded Lone Pine businessman. He was also an amateur astronomer. Probasco enjoyed the clear unclouded skies of the Owens Valley and bought a telescope so he, his family and friends could view the moon and stars through the clear desert air. Probasco soon concluded his new telescope could also work quite efficiently in the daytime as well. On his own ascent of Mt. Whitney, he planted a US flag at its summit and was intrigued when he saw he could view the flag through his telescope when he returned to Lone Pine.

Figure 48-The Lone Pine Observatory offered tourists glimpses of climbers on Mt. Whitney. A bakery and café operated in the building below

Probasco built a domed structure on top of his business, which was mounted onto rollers that would allow the dome to rotate 360°. On one side of the dome was a V-shaped opening, from which his telescope could be directed for closer viewing of a variety of subjects, the most popular of which was the summit of Mt. Whitney.

Probasco was able to rig a camera to the telescope, enabling him to take long distance pictures of the multitude of tourists and locals who scrambled their way to the top of the towering peak. The indisputable evidence his pictures provided of these would be mountaineer's accomplishments became enormously popular and helped fuel a very successful business at the restaurant and bakery he operated in the building below. His telescope was even featured in a story in the Los Angeles Times.

When Probasco passed away, his family sold the telescope to Ellis Sterling. Sterling operated a service station and garage in Lone Pine and the telescope continued to be a very popular tourist attraction for many more years.

Like many man-made attractions, Probasco's telescope has come and gone. But the mountaineering accomplishments of hundreds of alpinists can still be remembered in a few old faded photos and in our distant memory of William Probasco's Lone Pine Observatory.

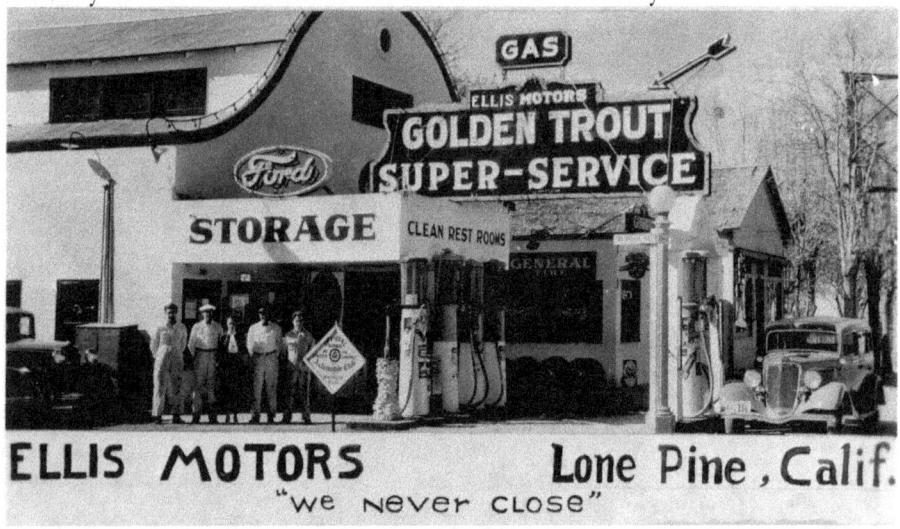

Figure 49-The Observatory was sold to Ellis Sterling, owner of famous Golden Trout Super-Service, a popular Lone Pine stop along El Camino Sierra

CHAPTER SEVENTEEN

COLD WAR IN THE EASTERN SIERRA

Many of us oldsters remember well the tense reality of living with life during the cold war of the 1950s and '60s. The newspapers reported another successful nuclear test by the Soviet Union on what seemed like a monthly basis. Teachers had their students practice duck and cover drills in their classroom with the regularity of homework, and most of us knew someone that had converted their basement into a bomb shelter. In the peaceful Owens Valley of the Eastern Sierra, reminders of the country's collective efforts to be prepared for the worst, were quietly present as well.

Just north of the Inyo County Courthouse in Independence, is the County Administrative Building. A few Inyo County government offices are here, as well as the chamber the Inyo County Board of Supervisors meets in most every Tuesday.

The concrete building has a 1960s vintage look to it. Its simple concrete design is rather unremarkable but the story behind the building is nothing short of implausible

Title Insurance and Trust Company was a huge Southern California based title company. It had been handling real estate transactions since the late 1800s and needless to say, the company had a huge inventory of documents associated with the title search work they had performed for decades. By the early 1960s, most of the company's records and documents had been converted to microfilm.

Title Company executives became concerned whether their massive amount of important records and documents were safe. With the films kept in a huge store room at their main offices in downtown Los Angeles, Title Company executives felt there was a real possibility of having their massive collection of records destroyed, in the event of a nuclear attack on Southern California.

One of the company executives liked to vacation in the Eastern Sierra and was well familiar with its remote nature. At a company board meeting, he proposed Title Insurance and Trust Company consider building a secure storage facility in unassuming Independence and house their collection of microfilm and documents there. The board agreed, and in 1961, their new building, just north of the Inyo County Courthouse was complete, and the records of the company were moved out of the crosshairs of a Soviet nuclear attack to the safety of Independence.

Figure 50-Inyo County Administrative Building & Board Chamber

The trust company's microfilm and documents were safely housed in their new concrete structure for a number of years. But as world tensions lessened and having to deal for years with the inconvenience of important documents needed for their work being located over four hours away, Title Insurance and Trust decided to bring all their records back to Los Angeles.

The title company put the building up for sale and eventually, a delightful little restaurant known as Anna's Italian Villa opened in the old bomb safe storage structure. The good folks of Independence enjoyed superb Italian cuisine for a number of years.

Alas…Anna's eventually closed down and after sitting vacant for a few years Inyo County purchased the building. It was first used for storage, and eventually turned into the County Administrative Office and Supervisor's Chambers it is today.

Hopefully someday we'll have eternal peace throughout the world and reminders of a more unsettled time…will just be another distant memory, here and elsewhere, along El Camino Sierra.

CHAPTER EIGHTEEN
MOVING WATER

A tale was often repeated during the early days around Virginia City and Carson City. It was said the wastes of Washoe were so barren that wild animals, including the formidable grizzly bear, gazed eastward from the heights of the Sierra Nevada, sniffed the acrid air and quickly turned west back into the sanctuary of Tahoe's well-watered forests.

Folk lore or not, it is quite true that the land east of the Sierra crest averages a fraction of the precipitation received in the mountains just a few miles to the west.

The discovery of gold and silver at the Comstock Lode in 1859, set forth one of the greatest boom towns the U.S. has ever seen. By the 1870s, the population of Virginia City and the surrounding towns was estimated to be over 25,000 inhabitants. The town already had a reputation for being a thirsty place, but it was parched with another thirst that all the whiskey in the West could not quench.

The valuable silver and gold had to be extracted from the ore taken from the ground. The complicated process required millions of gallons of water each day. The good citizens of Virginia City needed water to cook, and though hard to believe, the miners were also known to take an occasional bath as well as a drink of water.

At first, the few springs on the arid slopes of the Virginia Range supported the townspeople and the mining, but as the town grew, it became quite evident a great deal more H2O would be required if the town were ever to reach its obvious potential.

In 1872, the Virginia and Gold Hill Water Company sent out engineer H. Schussler to find a new water source to solve their shortage of liquid gold. Schussler felt the water flowing from the east slope of the Sierra Nevada Mountains was just the right solution to their shortage.

Franktown (now known as Hobart) Creek lies a mere 12 miles as the crow flies from the bustling Nevada metropolis. Its ample flow could significantly impact the town's water deficit. Just one major challenge…the water would have to be "lifted" over 1,400' to get over the mountains to Virginia City.

Figure 51-Hermann Schussler

Schussler already had a reputation as a very qualified engineer. He had designed the Spring Valley Water Works of San Francisco before the silver barons brought him to the Comstock. As a side note, the two earthen dams Schussler had constructed for water storage above San Francisco, easily withstood the great 1906 earthquake.

Schussler built a diversion dam high up on Hobart Creek. This high elevation reservoir combined with a box flume and pressure pipe, inverted siphon design, was the most elaborate water system ever attempted up to that time. Wrought iron pipe would need to be constructed to withstand the tremendous pressure of the water dropping nearly 2,000 vertical feet before it began its 1,400' climb to Virginia City.

Thirteen deep ravines or canyons would need to be crossed in the course of the new pipeline. Workers had a 30" trench dug by spring of 1873 and the first pipe was laid on June 11. By the 25th of July, in only six short weeks, Schussler and his men had completed the mind-bending project.

Water was brought from the storage reservoir to the pipe inlet by wooden box flume. Once it exited the pipe on the east side of the Virginia Mountain Range, the water would be carried the remaining seven miles in yet more flumes. The seven miles of 12" diameter steel pipe was constructed in 26' long sections, in thicknesses ranging from one sixteenth to five sixteenths. The total pipe weighed an astounding 700 tons and was hauled to the site by the Virginia & Truckee (V&T) Railroad. There were

1,524 fitted joints secured by a like number of metal connector rings. One million rivets were used, and thirty-five tons of lead poured for caulking.

When the water company opened the valves in Virginia City, a huge celebration began. Whistles at the mines and cannon fire from the militia announced to the world Virginia City had water. A torchlight parade passed through the city over and over till the break of dawn.

Figure 52-A wooden box flume was an instrumental part of the well-designed water system.

It is said there was only one flaw with the system. A pencil size hole on one section of the pipe grew to three inches in a matter of moments once the system was put under pressure. A jet of water spurted two hundred feet into the air from the hole. It was reported that the pressure of the escaping water was so great that it tuned a man's fingernails down as though he had held them against a spinning emery wheel.

The increase in available water led of course to an increase in demand. Virginia City continued to grow and in less than three years, more water was needed than the new system could deliver. In 1876, a second pipe was laid parallel to the original system, significantly increasing available water for the Comstock. Over the next few years, the system was expanded even further, bringing water from higher up the mountain at Marlette Lake.

The 21-mile water delivery system was so well designed, the basis of it is still providing water to the residents of Virginia City and Gold Hill today. The historic system is now managed and owned by Storey County.

Figure 53-Marlette Lake (center) sits in the Carson Range high above Lake Tahoe (bottom of photo)

Figure 54-Virginia City reached its massive potential thanks to the waters brought to it from the High Sierra

CHAPTER NINETEEN
THE HUBCAP QUEEN

Motorists making their way north from southern California along El Camino Sierra, crack a smile of alleviation as they see the convivial 18-foot-tall Uniroyal Girl of Pearsonville acting as a beacon guiding the traveler through the gateway into Eastern California.

The champagne-haired, red skirted, fiberglass effigy of allurement has been denoting the location of what at one time was the largest collection of hubcaps in the world for over 50 years.

In 1960, Andy and Lucy Pearson moved into a drafty two room shack located on 40 acres they had just purchased on the Inyo/Kern County line. Their dream was to build a roadside business marketed toward the Eastern Sierra traveler by offering homestyle cooking, gasoline, a kiddie playground, towing, an auto repair and a huge water tank.

The Pearson's operation also sold tires. During the mid-1960s, the Uniroyal Tire Company would partner with some of its dealerships placing a huge fiberglass statue they named the Uniroyal Girl at the dealer's location. It was claimed the sculptor modeled his work after Jackie Kennedy-Onassis. Uniroyal had dozens of these giant girls made to promote their tires and the ladies graced highways across the United States.

By the mid-1970s, the Pearsons had turned their operation into a full-fledged town dubbed Pearsonville, with one of the largest wrecking yards in the region. The family built the Pearsonville Raceway on a portion of their desert land, which for a number of years, attracted fast race cars and their drivers from all over the state. The U.S. Postal Service even gave Pearsonville its own zip code.

According to the Pearson's daughter Janice, her mom Lucy started collecting hubcaps to "keep herself busy." As Lucy's hobby began to turn into an obsession with the number of hubcaps totaling over 200,000, Andy confided to his daughter, "the old lady's lost her mind." Lucy became known far and wide as the Hubcap Queen and was featured on several TV shows including *To Tell the Truth*.

The Pearsons eventually retired and their grandchildren ran the business for a few more years. But with newer cars less prone to breakdowns and not needing fuel as often as the gas guzzling behemoths of the sixties and seventies, the operation came to an end, with the salvage yard being relocated to Ridgecrest and most of Lucy's beloved hubcaps turned into scrap metal.

Figures 55-Uniroyal Girl at Pearsonville & 56-(below) Pearsonville 1960s

Some folks may make light of Lucy Pearson and her passion for collecting hubcaps. But there's not many of us that have a world's record of anything, or a town named after us for that matter. Eastern Sierra history has certainly provided us with many colorful characters…here in bygone days of travel…along El Camino Sierra.

CHAPTER TWENTY
LONE PINE STAMPEDE

Inyo County has a long history of ranching and cowboying. In the early 1860s, the first settlers in the Owens Valley raised cattle for the mining camp of Aurora, and bronco-busting cow poking has held fast ever since.

In 1941, Lone Pine rancher and southern Inyo County legend Russell Spainhower, started the ball rolling for what became a yearly western event. Spainhower, working with stockman Wilfred Cline and community members from Lone Pine, created the Lone Pine Stampede, a rodeo held to celebrate southern Inyo's cowboy and ranching heritage.

At first, the Lone Pine Stampede was held on what was known as the town ball park. As it grew, a formal rodeo grounds was constructed in an open field behind where Lone Pine's Western Film History Museum stands today. A sturdy grandstand was built that would seat hundreds of spectators comfortably.

Rodeo events included calf roping, bareback riding, team roping, saddle-bronc riding, and bulldogging. Later years included presentations by the Bishopettes (a women's western riding club based in Bishop) and a water ski act held on nearby Diaz Lake south of town. By 1955, the Stampede program included Lone Pine versus Independence baseball, a parade, the Stampede dance, and of course…the coronation of a Stampede Queen. An early 1960's program lists a, "businessmen's burro race" as a stimulating part of the annual weekend.

Many years of celebrations hosted a wide range of activities in conjunction with the rodeo. First class parade competitions for prizes, with as many as seven marching bands performing and trophies in up to 19 categories; whiskerino (whisker growing) contests with intense rivalry sponsored by the Lions Club; and popular pet parades for the kiddies. Carnivals too came to the rodeo and added to the fun and excitement. Barbecues of the highest quality were staged by local organizations and drew hundreds of guests.

Slim Pickens was a rodeo clown for numerous Lone Pine Stampedes before his Hollywood acting career took off. Sponsors included the local

Lloyd's Shoe Store, Joseph's BiRite Market, the Lone Pine-J.C. Penney store and Wrangler Jeans.

Figure 57-Slim Pickens was a rodeo clown for the Lone Pine Stampede before his movie acting career took off

In 1963, due to the increasing costs of procuring stock and professional riders, the event changed to amateur status. Organizers kept the rodeo going for several more years but eventually, the Lone Pine Stampede faded into the sunset in 1980.

There are still many folks that fondly remember this classic piece of the Eastern Sierra's western history. It's been reported…the Museum of Western Film History's staff, with community encouragement and support, hopes to bring the beloved event back someday.

Figure 58-A Stampede program from 1946

CHAPTER TWENTYONE
FLYING HIGHEST

The varied and unique landscape of El Camino Sierra area has many attractions to it. The soaring mountains, deep canyons, lush forests and abundance of water offer a broad appeal to many diverse interests. Hikers, skiers, anglers, hunters, four-wheel drive enthusiasts, water seekers and researchers have all found the Eastern Sierra a perfect location to pursue their interests.

A bit south and west of the town of Bishop lies a very high spur ridge extending at an angle from the Sierra Nevada crest, that has its own unique appeal. Called Coyote Flat, the area is known for its jaw dropping views looking straight into this jagged section of the Sierra Nevada Mountains. The views of the Palisade Glacier area are particularly impressive.

The summit region of Coyote Flat reaches over 10,000 feet with much of the terrain relatively level. The area attracts outdoor enthusiasts who use a rough jeep road from Bishop to access this high alpine fairyland. Dispersed camping is very popular along this Eastern Sierra gem.

Coyote Flat's 10,000-foot elevation and reasonably level terrain attracted the U.S. Military's interest for a number of years during the mid-20th century. The high elevation and remote location made a perfect spot to construct an airfield for the purpose of conducting secret experimental aircraft test flights by the military and its contractors.

Because of the secret nature of the work done here, there is not a large amount of specific information available about Coyote Flat's use. The testing primarily involved an aircraft's ability to take off and land at such high elevation and the "Flat" was the highest airfield in the United States.

Helicopter use by the military was introduced on a very limited basis near the end of World War II. Their strategic and combat advantages were quite evident, and the U.S. Army initiated an ambitious development program for the new flying machine with its military contractors.

In the 1950s and '60s, prototypes of a variety of the new "whirlybirds" were observed flying in the airspace around Bishop and the nearby Sierra Nevada Mountains. A Cessna YH-41 helicopter was confirmed to have used the airy facility in 1958.

Figure 59-Coyote Ridge has a fairly level summit area and offers jaw dropping views of the nearby Sierra Nevada Mountains.

As technology in aircraft continued to develop, so did the use of Coyote Flat. The Army, Air Force and Marines along with aviation contractors began to use the area for not only testing, but training of their pilots and crews as well. In 1965, the military brought a huge CH-47 "Porky" and its crew up to Coyote Flat for flight testing. The Boeing built heavy lift was known as a Chinook and its enormous size introduced a new area in helicopter operations.

In 1965, the Army High Altitude Test Center announced in an official press release that it had built a 3,000' runway at Coyote Flat to, "test the high-altitude performance of helicopters and light airplanes." The press release went on to state the runway would also be used by the Marine Corps Mountain Warfare School in Bridgeport, California and that a secondary site in in the nearby White Mountains would also be used.

There is some debate about the exclusivity of Coyote Flat's use for only "light" airplanes. According to aviation historian Jed Keck, the Air Force even landed a C-130 Hercules transport at the rarified airfield. The Air Force website states the C-130 requires 3,250' of runway for lift-off. Must have been a thrilling experience to fly into the wild blue yonder from the Coyote Flat airfield in such a large plane.

Figure 60-Air Force evaluation crew in front of their CH-47, "Porky" at Coyote Flat, 1965

Figure 61-It's reported the U.S. Air Force even landed a C-130 at the high-altitude runway of Coyote Flat

Arial photos taken during the 1970's and '80s show a small building adjacent to the runway. Though there was never a permanent base at Coyote Flat, apparently crews were billeted in temporary camps for short periods of time to conduct their tests.

Figure 62-Coyote Flat airfield a few years after the military ceased use

The Coyote Flat airfield was evidently closed at some point between 1998-99, as it was no longer depicted at all (even as an abandoned airfield) on a 1998 World Aeronautical Chart or the 2000 Sectional Chart.

The property is now solely under the jurisdiction of the U.S. Forest Service and to discourage landings by civilian pilots, the Forest Service dug deep ruts into the runway and placed branches across it in an x-shaped pattern to ward off potential landings. The branches were later replaced by white rocks.

There is still a lot of interest in Coyote Flat by pilots evidenced by the amount of banter on the web about the possibility of landing there, but officially…the Coyote Flat Airfield is closed…and a nearly forgotten thrill in the memories of the daring pilots that flew here.

CHAPTER TWENTYTWO

FREMONT'S LOST CANNON

Captain John C. Fremont was an eminent explorer of the American West. Having joined the United States Topographical Corps in 1833, Fremont spent the next nine years surveying new railroad routes through the Appalachia Mountains. During his time in the eastern wilderness Fremont longed to become an explorer of unchartered lands.

In 1842, advocates of western expansionism in the US government chose Fremont to lead a scientific expedition to explore the Oregon Trail and report back on the fertility of its lands. Fremont followed the Oregon Trail west and originally had planned to return by the same route. But after arriving in Oregon, Fremont made the decision to return by a different route, one that would take him south into the Great Basin of Nevada in search of the purported river believed by many to cross the Sierra Nevada mountains to the Pacific Ocean.

Being a military man, Fremont wanted to be sufficiently armed to defend his expedition from any hostile activity they might encounter. In addition to plenty of small arms and ammunition, Fremont wanted to take along a mountain howitzer, partly to show that a wheel mounted vehicle could be taken through the mountain and desert trails where none had ever traveled before. The 223-pound bronze cannon provided to Fremont was cast in Massachusetts and could be towed by a horse or mule.

Fremont's expedition made their way south, exploring along the base of the Eastern Sierra Nevada. Running desperately short of supplies, the legendary scout Kit Carson led Fremont and his beleaguered men in a winter crossing over a pass in the Sierra Nevada Mountains to Sutter's Fort at Sacramento, where they obtained food and regained their strength.

Burdened by trying to move the heavy cannon through deep snow during his Sierra crossing, Fremont abandoned the piece of artillery on the east slope of the Sierras. For years, the cannon was never reclaimed and became the subject of numerous legends as to its whereabouts. It eventually became known as "Fremont's Lost Cannon." Lost Cannon Peak and Lost Cannon Canyon near Sonora Junction took their names from this legend.

Treasure hunters and historians searched the area near the West Fork of the Walker River for years in hopes of finding the lost Fremont artifact. Archeologists found what some believe is the barrel of Fremont's cannon in the Walker River area. Years later, researchers working with the United States Forest Service found parts of what they believe is the original "Lost Fremont Cannon." Both discovery sites are in the nearby vicinity of where Fremont's records say he abandoned it back in 1844. All these parts are on display and can be enjoyed at the Nevada State Museum in Carson City.

And Fremont's Lost Cannon lives on today in the football rivalry between the University Nevada Reno (UNR) and University Nevada Las Vegas (UNLV). The brainchild of UNLV's first football coach Bill Ireland, who thought the two teams needed a special trophy for the winner of their yearly football contest to display. A replica of Fremont's original howitzer was chosen. Kennecott Copper Company built and donated the cannon which cost over $10,000 and at 545 pounds, is the most expensive and heaviest trophy in college football. Originally, the cannon was fired after every touchdown of the team in possession.

Figure 63-A replication of Fremont's 1844 Lost Cannon

Whether the parts found are truly the "Lost Fremont Cannon" or not is still not known with complete certainty, but the tale of this piece of Eastern Sierra history lives on here, along El Camino Sierra.

CHAPTER TWENTYTHREE

TEX CUSHION AND HIS SLED DOGS

By 1927, the mining boom that was Mammoth City and the Lake Mining District had been over for nearly 40 years. Most of the folks that still lived in the area made their living from logging and from the few hardy tourists who made their way to the area to fish during the summer.

Few people actually lived in Mammoth during the winter months. No snow plows cleared the roads and snowmobiles were something that existed only on the drawing boards of engineers. Getting around in Mammoth during the winter was a very difficult proposition.

Canadians Tex and Ruth Cushion came to Mammoth from Quebec that winter of 1927. Tex had operated dog teams back in Canada and shortly after they arrived in Mammoth, the Cushions acquired a dog team to help them stay mobile during the long Sierra winter.

Tex's ability to get around with his dogs even during the most trying of winter conditions soon became legendary. Blizzards struck often in the Mammoth area, concealing all land forms and markers. Despite the conditions, Tex always seemed to be able to make his way around. He maintained a regular patrol to the remote caretaker cabins up in the Lake's Basin, bringing supplies and mail when others would not even venture outside. He even carried needed supplies in winter to a remote mining camp over Minaret Summit and beyond Devil's Postpile. Tex recalled he once used 23 dogs to haul 1,500 pounds of supplies and equipment to the mining camp. The lead dog was an astounding 94 feet in front of Tex and his sled.

Tex's work also included removing snow from the roofs of summer cabins. The Cushions would employ several people to help them with their work including taking care of the sled dogs at their kennel. Alaskan Malamutes became the breed the Cushions favored and the fine canines they raised were sought by sledders and mushers from throughout the western U.S.

Each spring, Tex would take a team of dogs and gear to the Automobile Club of Southern California's Outdoor Show in Los Angeles. His dogs found the sunny and warm Southern California weather a bit difficult to handle at times. Tex would often contract with a local ice house to bring in blocks of ice to the show to keep his dogs cool. The famed musher and his canines were among the most popular attractions at the shows.

Figure 64-Ted and Ruth Cushion's Mammoth Sled Dog office

Hollywood movie studios would make occasional trips to Mammoth Lakes during winter to shoot a perfect snowy scene for a feature film. Tex and his crew would transport the movie crews, actors and all their gear to various snowbound locations throughout the Mammoth area to get their winter shot.

Longtime Mammoth resident Nan Zischank recalled, "One day, Tex answered the telephone and it was Barney Johnson from Crystal Crag Resort. Johnson said, "My dog team will be coming down the trail past you in about five minutes, Tex. Please stop the so and soes! I harnessed them and forgot to hook them to the sled. When I yelled mush, they took off and there I stood on the sled while the dogs ran off down the trail." Sure enough, the dogs made it on time and Tex corralled them in.

The Cushions were also quite accomplished skiers. They were as comfortable on the skinny boards as they were behind their dog teams. Ruth and Tex were instrumental in working with Dave McCoy and others in forming the first organized ski area in the Mammoth area at McGee Mountain. Tex also originated the popular costumed Easter Egg Hunt on Skis which was an Eastern Sierra ski area tradition for many years.

Figure 65-Mammoth Mountain founders Dave & Roma McCoy shown participating in the costumed "Easter Egg Hunt on Skis," originated by Tex Cushion

Innumerable desperate situations during a Mammoth Lakes' winter were avoided thanks to Tex, Ruth and their dogs. In times of heavy snow, they would take the sick or injured residents to wherever Highway 395 was open, which sometimes was all the way to the top of Sherwin Grade, where a doctor from Bishop would meet them to care for the patient.

Figure 66-Tex and Ruth Cushion and their dogs were often the only mode of travel in the Mammoth area during the winter months

Many brave people have lived here in the Eastern Sierra, giving generously of themselves to help their fellow man and woman. In the case of Tex and Ruth Cushion, they did so with the help of man's best friend…which carried them over an often snow covered…El Camino Sierra.

Figure 67 & 67A (below)-Tex Cushion near Mammoth Lakes with his dogs

CHAPTER TWENTYFOUR
FROM THE HALLS OF PICKEL MEADOWS

California State Highway 108, also known as the Sonora Pass Road, is unquestionably one of the most scenic drives not just in California, but in the entire United States.

Travelers along this remote byway are often surprised to come upon a modern looking facility, complete with apartments, industrial looking buildings and a landing strip, nestled against the backdrop of majestic Sierra Nevada peaks. This would be the location of the United States Marine Corps' Pickel Meadows training camp.

The United States Marine Corps began training in this Toiyabe National Forest location in 1951 during the Korean War. The harsh winter conditions on the Korean Peninsula caught the leathernecks unprepared and the Marine command at Camp Pendleton near San Diego, established the Pickel Meadows Training Camp designating it the "Cold Weather Battalion, Staging Regiment, Training and Replacement Command." The camp immediately became the location for all cold-weather training for Marines headed to Korea.

The Marines quickly built a few temporary buildings and erected about 50 tents for billeting, which were soon replaced with permanent structures. The facility proved invaluable in preparing the brave Marines in their determined defense of South Korea.

That winter of 1951-52 was a tough one. A Southern Pacific passenger train became snowbound and unable to move for 10 days near Donner Pass due to the exceptionally deep snow. Marines at Pickel Meadows experienced similar conditions as snowdrifts piled higher and higher at the base, burying vehicles and equipment. By mid-January, California snow plow crews were unable to keep Highway 395 open beyond the town of Bishop, causing the Pickel Meadows base to become completely isolated for almost a week. As food and stove oil began to run low, the Marines sent C-119 cargo planes that parachuted critically needed supplies to the 1,500 trainees who were snowbound at the base.

Realizing the relevant training conditions the base provided, the Marine Corps continued with winter training at Pickel Meadows after the end of the Korean War. By 1963, the facility's mission was expanded to include mountain warfare training for the leathernecks, and the camp became known as the Marine Corps Mountain Warfare Training Center.

Figure 68-The Marine's Pickel Meadow facility has been training leathernecks in mountain warfare skills since the early 1950s.

During the Vietnam War, most of the camp's trainers were needed directly in combat and the base was temporarily closed in 1967. Once the war was over, the Marines reopened Pickel Meadows for mountain warfare training in 1976.

Today the Pickel Meadows facility plays an important role in preparing Marines to deal with a wide range of extreme conditions they may encounter someday. The camp and its soldiers are good neighbours as well, adopting Highway 108 and the surrounding area as their own. Troops can often be seen clearing drainage culverts, cutting brush, policing for trash and performing other repairs and improvements to the area's roadways and infrastructure.

We have much to enjoy here in the land of the free and the home of the brave...and we hope the courageous men and women who help make our freedom possible...are enjoying their time at what may be one of the most scenic military facilities anywhere...located just a few miles west...of El Camino Sierra.

CHAPTER TWENTYFIVE

MINT CONDITION

It seems like these days, the use of coins as part of our everyday currency is about as antiquated as using a rotary dial phone. Many people look at the heavy, bulky pennies, nickels, dimes and quarter as more of a nuisance than an asset, but they have long been an important part of history here in the Eastern Sierra.

The U.S. has been minting coins since 1792, and during the entire history of the United States, there have only been eight cities that have had the honor of being home to a U.S. Mint. Carson City, Nevada is one of those prestigious locales and the history of the Carson City Mint is an interesting tale.

By the early 1860s, the mines of the famous Comstock Lode of Virginia City were producing gold and silver in huge quantities. At that time, the closest mint that could process the precious minerals into coinage was in San Francisco…a fairly short drive today but a difficult and dangerous trip back in 1863. Congress made the decision to build a mint in Carson City, a mere 15 miles from the Comstock, to mint the gold and silver into coin.

The Civil War delayed the start of construction at the new Carson City Mint, but fifteen months after the war had ended, the official plans for the town's new mint arrived in Carson City and the local newspaper proclaimed, "A Glorious Day for Carson! The Arrival of the Mint Papers!!—Joy and Gunpowder!!!"

The cornerstone was laid by September of 1866, but the actual construction went very slowly over the next four years. Carson City founder Abe Curry had been instrumental in getting Congress to choose their town for the mint. As funds from the government for construction were very slow in arriving, Curry often paid many expenses for the new mint out of his own pocket. The situation became so desperate Curry had to file for bankruptcy because he had put out so much of his own funds to try and get the mint built. After several delays and restarts, the U.S. Government's Carson City Mint opened on February 4th of 1870. The final cost was $425,000.

Figure 69-Abe Curry, the founder of Carson City was instrumental in bringing the mint to his town

Unfortunately, once the mint was finally open, significant new challenges surfaced. The kings of the Comstock Lode, John McKay, William O'Brien, James Flood and James Fair preferred to send their bullion to the San Francisco Mint for processing. All four had major real estate investments in California, and they found it more profitable to have their valuable ore minted in the City by the Bay.

Despite the challenges, the Carson City Mint plugged along until 1885, when Democrat Grover Cleveland became president. He was the first Democrat in the White House since Nevada became a state in 1864. This election was correctly seen as a threat to the livelihood of the mint's officers, all of whom were faithful members of the Republican Party. The mint was indeed closed just a few months after Cleveland was elected and its officers all replaced.

In 1888, Republican Benjamin Harrison was elected President and the Carson City Mint's staff of Democratic political appointees were dispatched and again replaced with victorious Republicans. Republicans appropriated the necessary funding and the mint was reopened and back in business by July 1, 1889. It ran at full capacity for the next three years.

One of the more interesting bits of history at the mint is the significant contribution women made, working in jobs from quality control to operating coin presses and milling machines. Women adjusters were responsible for making sure the coin blanks, known as planchets, were the exact weight required for minting. After handling thousands of planchets, the women developed such a sensitivity they could file the tiniest bits of gold or silver off to reach the correct weight, all without using a scale.

The women wore leather aprons to collect the valuable gold and silver dust, and each year in June, there was an accounting of how much precious metal dust was recovered. This was sent to the mint director to show just how efficient and successful the adjusters were in their efforts to conserve the valuable minerals. They even burned their clothing periodically, just to collect any gold and silver residue.

Figure 70-The Mint brought prestige and recognition to the state capital

In 1892, Grover Cleveland won an unprecedented second and nonsequential presidential term, and combined with the declining production of the Comstock Lode, the mint breathed a final breath. The last coins produced were in June of 1893, but the building was repurposed and operated as the U.S. Assay Office for northern Nevada.

Carson City-ites kept up hope the mint itself would somehow reopen, but in 1895, an investigation revealed that $80,000 worth of gold bullion had been embezzled at the mint during its final years. Two men were charged and eventually found guilty. In 1933, the Great Depression brought on the closure of the building for good. Or did it?

District Court Judge Clark Guild enjoyed going for morning walks through the streets of Carson City. He would often notice the dilapidated old federal building as he made his way along the state capital's streets. A native Nevadan with a life dedicated to public service, Judge Guild pondered the notion the old mint might be a suitable location for the Nevada State Museum he had been promoting. Thanks to his efforts, the state purchased the closed mint for $5,000 and began the arduous task of putting together a state museum. On October 31, (Nevada Day) 1941, the former mint proudly reopened its doors…this time as the new Nevada State Museum. Judge Guild stayed active with the museum, building, growing, collecting and finding new supporters up until his death in 1971.

Nevadans were proud of the new home for their state's history and heritage. Tens of thousands of people a year enjoyed the many interpretive exhibits and displays. Over the years, the museum has expanded to include the original historic mint building, the Calhoun Annex that was added in the 1970s, and a separate building to the north, which was purchased in 2004. In 2009, a beautiful concourse was built to link the three buildings and give access to all five floors for those with mobility concerns. One of the most popular exhibits at the state museum is the interpretive display of the old mint itself, located in the original mint building,

The showpiece of the Nevada State Museum today is massive coin press #1. Visitors can marvel at the six-ton monolith as it produces half-dollar size coins on the last Friday of every month. When the Carson City Mint closed, the historic press was moved first to the San Francisco Mint and later to the Philadelphia Mint. It finally came home to the old Carson City Mint/Nevada State Museum in 1955. It came to the aid of the U.S. Treasury again in 1964, when facing a severe coin shortage, the Director of the U.S. Mint requested the use of the press again. It was transported to the Denver Mint for three years where it dutifully produced millions of dollars of U.S. coins before returning to its Nevada Museum home, where it is still proudly on display today.

Figure 71-Carson City Mint Coin Press #1

CHAPTER TWENTYSIX

LADY ON THE FLYING SKIS

The Eastern Sierra has long been home to strong willed women and men. Strength and perseverance are common denominators of many a pioneer, who found their place in life…unfettered by the many challenges they faced in the Eastern Sierra.

Nan Conner was born to a wealthy family in Columbus, Ohio in 1907. Her father Wayne Conner was the manager of the Rexall Drug medicinal factory. The family eventually moved to Southern California, which is where Nan met hard working gas station attendant Max Zischank, whom she married in 1931.

With unbridled enthusiasm and optimism, the young couple struck out to make their fortune in the frontier town of Mammoth Lakes, with only their car, Inky their dog and $50 in cash.

Nan and Max were quickly hired to work at Mammoth's legendary Penny's Tavern and also became the winter caretakers at Tamarack Lodge. The voluminous amounts of snow they dealt with in the Mammoth Lakes Basin quickly taught the energetic couple some lessons in winter survival.

Nan and Max met neighbors Tex and Ruth Cushion (see chapter 21). Tex was French Canadian and was a master of making the best of living in a wintery climate. Tex had rigged up a simple rope tow on a nearby hillside, where Nan soon began developing her skiing technique. The Zischanks and Cushions spent many a winter night building their friendship around a roaring fireplace. The two couples became lifelong friends.

With the death of her father in 1937, Nan inherited $7,000. Nan and Max purchased a 125-foot building leftover from the Los Angeles Department of Water and Power's nearby Mono Craters tunnel construction project. Max sawed a 25' section off for his friend Tex to use as an addition to his cabin, and eventually brought the remainder of the building to property he and Nan had bought in Long Valley, and thus began Long Valley Resort.

Figure 72-Nan Zischank

When Nan and Max spent their first winter caretaking Tamarack Lodge and learning to ski, Tex had told Nan she had a natural ability and should work at really developing her skiing skills. When they built their Long Valley Resort, they soon erected a modest rope tow nearby, which Nan used on an almost daily basis.

About the same time, Dave McCoy, who later became the founder of Mammoth Mountain Ski Area, showed up on the scene, often using barrel staves to fly down the steep slopes of the Zischank's ski slope. The winter recreation scene in Mono County was starting to take off.

By 1941, Max and Nan were doing fairly well with their Long Valley Resort, catering to fishermen in the summer and the increasing number of recreationists during the snow-covered months of winter. But in December of 1941, Pearl Harbor was attacked and the Zischanks made a decision to close their resort and join the war effort. Max enlisted in the Army's Construction Battalion, 86th Division and was soon stationed at Adak Island, Alaska.

Nan got work as a security officer at Manzanar Internment Camp near Independence in the Owens Valley. One of Nan's primary duties was to transport Japanese internees who had received permission to relocate to inland areas of the United States. Nan drove the released internees from Manzanar in a small passenger bus to the railroad station in Reno, Nevada. From there, the displaced Japanese-Americans would take a train to their new homes away from the Pacific Coast. Nan made three 500-mile round trips a week to Reno the year round, logging nearly 170,000 miles. Nan was remembered by many of the Japanese Americans at Manzanar as a companion, guide, advisor, diplomat and friend.

Figure 73-Nan drove thousands of Japanese Americans to the railroad station in Reno, enabling them to leave Manzanar and relocate to areas in the central U.S.

During this time, Nan was able to make occasional stops while passing through the Mono County snow country, where she spent her time continuing to develop into a world class skier.

In 1942 the Automobile Club of Southern California sponsored an International Invitational Ski Race. Nine men and two women were invited to compete in the "Flying Skis" Carson Peak Run at June Lake. Most of the racers were European but two were from the Eastern Sierra. Nancy Zischank of Long Valley and Augie Hess of Lee Vining upheld the local honor.

The course was set down Devil's Chute. The Chute was just exactly that ...a long narrow channel on the face of Carson Peak, whose incline was so steep not a tree grew on it and whose sides were so close that the race course was set with tight turns almost straight down.

The morning of the race came, and Nan tied the skins to her skis and began the ascent several thousand feet above to the starting gate. Five hours later Nan reached the gate for the four-minute downhill run to the finish line. The skier before Nan crashed just in front of the finish gate, breaking his leg with eight spiral fractures. As Nan was fast approaching, the people at the bottom of the run were shouting, "Don't come down! Don't come down!" From high on the mountain Nan thought they were yelling, "Come on down! Come on Down!"…and she did. It wasn't until she was close to the downed skier, racing at top speed, that Nan saw the problem. She put herself into a slide, plowed under the injured skier and carried them both through the finish gate.

Figure 74-Nan Zischank-Lady on the Flying Skis

Nan and the other skier were taken in the back of a truck to Bridgeport on mattresses furnished by a local motel, and delivered into the competent hands of Dr. William Denton. Dr. Denton set the skier's broken leg and took several x-rays of Nan, pronouncing her whole. Getting up the next morning Nan found herself black and blue from head to toe and questioning the doctor's pronouncement, but for all of it, Nan had won the prestigious "Flying Skis" Trophy.

With the war nearly over, Max and Nan returned to their Long Valley Resort in spring of 1945. The Zischanks settled in to many years of offering exceptional hospitality and creating lifelong and memorable experiences for their guests at their beloved Mono County resort.

But in 1969, that would all change. During the infamous winter of that record setting year, snow had been falling nonstop in the entire Eastern Sierra for several days. A mountain of snow broke loose from the slopes above the Zischank's resort. When it hit the building, the snow blasted through the door. Max was carried still sitting in his chair, across the room and then buried in a debris pile of snow and glass. Nan was working in the kitchen several rooms away and escaped the avalanche's blast. She had to crawl along the three-foot space between the mound of snow and the ceiling of their living room to get to Max. Cut and bruised but otherwise not seriously hurt, Max and Nan safely escaped, but their Long Valley Resort was completely destroyed.

Not to be deterred, the Zischanks stayed in the Eastern Sierra and remained prominent members of their community for the remainder of their lives, helping Dave McCoy develop Mammoth Mountain into a world class destination ski area as well as playing an important role in a number of Eastern Sierra civic projects. Nan and Max Zischank have now skied on to the eternal black diamond run of life…but may the wonderful tales of these two giants of the Eastern Sierra live on in our memories forever, and inspire us to be our best, here along El Camino Sierra.

Figure 75-Nan and Max Zischank with Mammoth Mountain Dave McCoy

EASTERN CALIFORNIA MUSEUM

Special thanks to the Eastern California Museum in Independence, CA for providing reference and source material for a very large portion of the narrative and photos found in this book. A true Eastern Sierra treasure, stop in and enjoy this top-notch museum.
Open every day 10 am-5 pm. Closed major holidays.
155 N Grant St, Independence, California
http://www.inyocounty.us/ecmsite/ (760) 878-0364

CHAPTER TWENTYSEVEN

TOM'S PLACE

The first section of El Camino Sierra to be built was the roadway climbing from the Owens Valley to the top of Sherwin Grade. A great celebration of over 1,000 people was held in the meadows near the top of the grade. As soon as new roads were built in the Eastern Sierra, new businesses catering to the needs of motorists and travelers began to appear.

Just one year after the celebration at the top of Sherwin Grade, German born Hans Lof was traveling in the Eastern Sierra and thought the area near the site was the perfect spot to build a fuel station to take care of the hundreds of motorists who were now using the new El Camino Sierra to travel to the Eastern Sierra vacation lands.

Business was good from the start and Lof soon added a cookhouse and store. With a great number of travelers staying in the immediate area to fish and recreate nearby at Rock Creek, Lof acquired horses and pack animals, built a corral and began to offer guided pack trips into the Sierra wilderness surrounding Rock Creek.

Lof successfully operated his resort until 1923, when he sold the property to Thomas Yerby and his wife Hazel. Hazel was a Hollywood actress and went by the stage name of Jane Grey. The Yerbys bought Lof's successful road stop for $5,000 and continued to expand the resort. In 1924, they built a lodge for guests to stay, and renamed their resort, Tom's Place.

Down the road in Independence, the Mt. Whitney Fish Hatchery had just recently been completed and sport-fish stocking of Eastern Sierra creeks and lakes was well underway. Rock Creek was one of the prime locales for anglers to test their skills and at the same time, travelers were flocking to see the marvels of Yosemite National Park via the recently completed Tioga Pass Road...both bringing much traffic to Tom's Place.

A small forested flat of Forest Service land just a little west of Tom's Place was developed into the auto camp of French Camp. Visitors would come and camp for weeks at a time and helped to keep Tom's Place Resort busy during the entire summer. Business became so good that the Yerbys added tent structures and then permanent cabins. Some of these units are still in use today.

Figure 76-The original Tom's Place Resort

Hazel Yerby did most of cooking for the lodge. When prohibition ended in 1933, the Yerbys built a saloon across the highway. Hazel wouldn't let the saloon be on the same side of the street as the lodge and cafe.

Figure 77-Rock Creek Lake Resort was built further up Rock Creek Canyon and became another popular destination for anglers and adventurers

The 1930s were an active time in the Tom's Place area. Two resorts, Rock Creek Lodge and Rock Creek Lakes Resort were built further up Rock Creek Canyon. Construction workers building nearby Crowley Lake Dam and the Mono Craters tunnel helped keep Tom's Place busy. Despite the Great Depression and a World War, Tom's Place survived reasonably well.

Figure 78-Construction workers of the Crowley Lake Dam kept Tom's Place busy during the 1930s

Tom Yerby passed away in 1940. Hazel continued on as owner/manager of Tom's Place until 1945, when she sold it to Ted Berner and his family for $80,000. By this time, the state had paved the highway in front of the Resort and the future look pretty bright. That was, until a kitchen fire burned the old lodge to the ground in 1947.

Berner quickly rebuilt the Eastern Sierra landmark and moved the saloon inside the new main building. The rebuilt Tom's Place Resort is the same building still being used today.

A group of investors under the name Tomco, Inc purchased the Resort from the Berners in 1985. Tomco focused their efforts on the summer trade, offering only very limited services during the winter.

Since 2000, Mark and Michelle Layne, and their son Charlie have been the owners of this legendary property. They worked hard renovating and refurbishing their treasured resort, while maintaining its original ambiance and historical integrity. The Laynes continue Tom's Place long tradition of being a focal point of the local community, sponsoring car shows, BBQs, fundraisers and holiday parties...all while providing exceptional guest experiences to the Eastern Sierra visitor. In a world where things seem to change on an hourly basis, it's heartening to know there are still constants like Tom's Place, where welcoming hospitality and providing enduring fond memories to travelers and locals alike are still the foundation of this Eastern Sierra institution...for over one-hundred years.

Figure 79 and 80-Tom's Place Resort has been a welcoming landmark along El Camino Sierra for over 100 years

CHAPTER TWENTYEIGHT

RICHARD NEUTRA'S OYLER HOUSE

The scene driving west up the Whitney Portal Road from Lone Pine is one of dramatic landscapes of the highest order. The escarpment of the Sierra Nevada looms above like a mystical fortress while the close-up views of the aberrant shaped Alabama Hills entices the viewer to examine closer.

Nestled in the cottonwood trees along a particularly fascinating section of the Alabama Hills, lies a little-known piece of architectural excellence, the Oyler House.

Figure 81-Architect Richard Neutra

In 1957, Richard Oyler, Inyo County Tax Collector and resident of Lone Pine, came upon a *Time Magazine* article that featured modernist architect Richard Neutra, a student of Frank Lloyd Wright. Neutra was one of the most highly regarded architects in the U.S. at that time. He had even been recently featured in the Museum of Modern Art. Intrigued by his work, Oyler wrote to Neutra in 1959 to see if he would consider designing a modest home for him on property he owned in the Alabama Hills.

According to actress Kelly Lynch, who now owns the Oyler House, Neutra was taken aback by Oyler's incredible Alabama Hills property when he came to see it in person. He felt the inspiring Alabama Hills site would provide him the perfect canvas to create a masterpiece design. Neutra agreed to design a house for

Oyler and his family for a fee far below his customary compensation, and the two began a friendship that lasted for the next several years.

Neutra was known for his philosophy of "bio-realism." He created designs that integrated indoor and outdoor spaces, using glass walls and framing to bring features of the surrounding landscape into the buildings he designed. Neutra's style is clearly evident in his work at the Oyler House.

Neutra paired large glass walls with post and beam construction to allow the varied angles and features of the incredible landscape, to create the illusion that the indoor space extends forever into the surrounding scenery.

Neutra would often visit the Oylers at their home during the Christmas season, staying for a week or more at a time. Richard Oyler later recalled he felt Neutra enjoyed visiting the home he had so beautifully designed as much as he did the Oyler family.

In 2012, Richard Oyler's step-grandson, Mike Dorsey made a film titled, "The Oyler House: Richard Neutra's Desert Retreat," to tell the story of how Neutra came to build the Oyler's family home in Lone Pine. The documentary film is very well done and well worth seeing.

The home is private property and not open to the public. Please be respectful of the owners and stay out. But if you would like to know more about this beautiful piece of architecture found near El Camino Sierra, search the web for Dorsey's documentary.

Figure 82-View from the Oyler House

CHAPTER TWENTYNINE

CONVICT CASINO

The nation's penal system has experimented with a variety of programs to help rehabilitate and reform those that have run afoul of the law and are now incarcerated behind bars. From alligator control in Florida to snow removal in Montana, prison officials have tried almost everything to help inmates stay busy, learn important skills and develop self-worth.

It seems only fitting, that in the great state of Nevada, a method of recovery was set forth that followed closely along the lines of the Silver State's long history of gaming.

From 1932 to 1967, inmates at the Nevada State Maximum Security Prison in Carson City operated a gaming operation that offered blackjack, craps, poker, gin rummy and even sports betting…and they did so with the expressed approval and sanctioning of the warden and prison officials. The prison even checked the background of all gaming participants.

The prison casino was dubbed the "Bullpen" and was located in one of the old stone structures that dotted the venerable prison. The local Kiwanis Club and even department managers and employees from nearby state government offices would stop by the prison casino to try their luck.

Former Mustang Ranch brothel owner Joe Conforte, who is now a fugitive living in Brazil, was a dealer and croupier on some of the games during the time he spent at the prison in 1962, while serving a sentence for larceny.

Dennis Neilander was the chairman of the Nevada State Gaming Control Board from 2000-2010. He is quoted as saying, "It was a different time. They thought it would keep them out of trouble. It wouldn't happen today."

Prior to 1959, gaming control largely fell on county sheriffs and not the state. Local officials often made decisions on gaming that they felt were best for their locale. Nevada also had a long history of accepting and tolerating gambling, long before it became the first state to legalize gaming in 1931.

It was the opinion of some that inmates would gamble, regardless of whether it is legal or illegal and that by allowing sanctioned gambling, many

Figure 83-Inmates playing roulette in prison

inmates would stay out of trouble. Prison officials thought the games in prison would be more honest, because cheating inmates would be scared of the consequences.

The prison casino even had their own gaming tokens they referred to as "brass." The rare tokens are now highly valued by collectors, often times garnering $200 or more each.

Wardens often took a fair amount of heat from the community and the media for the casino. In 1957, after being called on the carpet again in yet another newspaper column, Warden Art Bernard told a reporter that it was impossible to prevent gambling by convicts and that the prison casino was supervised by prison guards. "These guys are experts," Bernard said about the casino convicts. "You can be sure they allow no cheating."

Each inmate who operated a game needed to have enough money to bankroll the game and receive the warden's approval. He also had to pay a fee of $25 to $75 per game every six months. The games were open to all inmates who stayed out of trouble, and outside guests were often invited to try their luck. Profits made from the gaming went to the prisoner welfare relief fund.

In 1967, the state of Nevada hired Carl Hocker, a transplant from the California prison system as the new warden in Carson City. Hocker was a little taken aback by the convict casino and brought an end to inmate gaming within a matter of weeks. He also sold off the gaming tokens.

"I think gambling in prison is a degradation, and it's certainly not constructive," Hocker is quoted as having said shortly after his arrival. "We're trying to replace it with constructive, wholesome activities that will contribute to a decent, healthful state of mind." Hocker's idea of wholesome activities were handicrafts, bridge, chess, ping-pong, volleyball, shuffleboard and making bead necklaces.

Figure 84-Joe Conforte (left) of the Mustang Ranch operated games at the Convict Casino in the early 1960s

There had been a riot at the prison in early 1967, shortly before the new warden arrived. Some state legislators were already up in arms about the prison sanctioning inmate gaming and had introduced a bill to bring the convict casino to an end. Hocker was coming from infamous San Quentin prison and already had a reputation as a strict disciplinarian.

The old Nevada State Prison was closed in 2011, but the Bullpen Casino lives on in these tales of history…and in the faded memories of those that were there.

Figure 85-The convict casino even had its own gaming tokens, known as "brass

CHAPTER THIRTY

A SIERRA WOODPECKER

The land along El Camino Sierra is renowned for the wide variety of wildlife that calls the mountains, streams and forests home. From the Clarks Nutcracker to the California Mule Deer to the famed Golden Trout, there is an abundance of fish, mammals and feathered creatures living in the shadow of these majestic mountains. There is a particular member of the bird family whose association with the Eastern Sierra, though not well known is intricately tied.

Walter Lantz was born in New York in 1899. Lantz was always interested in art, taking a mail order drawing class at age 12. His first job was as a newspaper cartoonist where he began experimenting with animation.

In 1927, he moved to California and was quickly hired by Universal Studios, where he developed the characters of Andy Panda, Winchester Tortoise and others. Lantz's career in animation continued to evolve, becoming an independent producer supplying cartoons to the studios instead of merely overseeing the animation department.

Figure 86-Walter Lantz, creator of Woody Woodpecker and benefactor of the Eastern Sierra

Lantz met the love of his life Grace Stafford and they were married in 1940. The June Lake area had already been a popular get-away for the Hollywood crowd, and Walter and Grace spent their honeymoon at Silver Lake Resort.

Walter told of how a noisy woodpecker kept the newlyweds annoyed with his antics including drilling holes in their cabin's roof, which allowed the afternoon rain to drip through onto their bed. Trying to calm her irritated husband, Grace proposed Walter develop a new cartoon character around the feathered fiend. Walter agreed and Woody Woodpecker made his hit debut in a 1941 animated short *Knock, Knock*. Mel Blanc was the original voice of Woody. Eventually Grace took over Woody's voice and she kept that job for the remainder of his career.

Despite or because of the infamous woodpecker experience they endured at Silver Lake, the Lantz's bought a home at the Sierra gem, where they vacationed for a good part of the summer for the next several decades. They spent so much time in the Eastern Sierra it became more than just a second home. The Lantz's loved the June Lake area and became important and active members of their community.

The Lantz's helped to fund the creation of the library in June Lake in 1962. Included in their generous support was an original oil painting Walter had created of Woody. In fact, Lantz provided original art work to a number of his June Lake friends and neighbors, many of which are still proudly displayed today. The Lantz's also provided the necessary funds for a ball field in the nearby town of Lee Vining. The Walter Lantz Field still provides recreational opportunities to the residents of this small town at the eastern entrance to Yosemite.

Figure 87-The Lantzs funded the ballfield in Lee Vining

CHAPTER THIRTYONE

SPARK PLUGS

The year was 1920. Dr. Joseph Jeffery steadied himself as he leaned out the door of the Carson & Colorado Railroad's freight car as the train passed along the base of White Mountain Peak. Jeffrey wanted to get off at an unscheduled stop and the engineer refused to halt the train but told Jeffery he would "slow the train a bit" at his desired spot. As the train slowed, Jeffery, with bag in hand...jumped from the railcar, landing on the dirt with a thud, but otherwise unhurt.

Dr. Jeffery was a dentist and also a trained mining engineer and geologist. He came to the Chalfant Valley northeast of Bishop, California searching for a rare mineral known as sillimanite. Sillimanite was the key ingredient that would make porcelains hard enough for dentures, as well as sparkplugs that could hold up to the heat of high-octane airplane fuel. After World War I had ended, the demand for the valuable mineral was high.

Figure 88-Dr. Joseph Jeffery

At the time, there were no known natural deposits of sillimanite in the entire country. Sillimanite could be made synthetically but the process of manufacturing it was very costly.

Jeffery felt certain there should be a deposit of sillimanite somewhere in nature and from his research and studies, it seemed probable that the right conditions might be found in the White Mountains of California.

Working with a local prospector, Dr. Jeffery hunted the steep slopes on the western flank of White Mountain. After much searching and exploring, most of the time dangling at the end of a rope while scouring a light-colored cliff, the diligent prospector yelled down to the good dentist… "Hey Doc…we found it!"

Find it they did…Dr Jeffery quickly filed patents on the site and bought the cattle ranch in the valley directly below. He hired several men to help him develop the deposit of the precious sillimanite. A steep trail to the mine was built and mules were used to haul the valuable mineral out. Each four-legged beast would carry 400 pounds of ore down the steep and difficult trail. Dr. Jeffery became the major provider of sillimanite for the largest spark plug manufacturer in the U.S. at that time, the Champion Spark Plug Company. His operation would come to be known as the Spark Plug Mine.

Figure 89-Dr. Jeffery sold most of the sillimanite to Champion Spark Plug

Supplies and equipment had to be carried up the same difficult and steep trail. The packers would disassemble heavy equipment down to their bare bones and carry the pieces up in sections. A walk-in refrigerator was carried up by its doors, sides, bolts, hinges and screws. The biggest challenge was a compressor. Every possible part was removed, but the basic unit still weighed a whopping 600 pounds. The packer chose "Old Maude," the strongest of the mules for the job. She plodded up the trail one hoof in front of the other. Upon her arrival at lower camp, the miners had to use a hoist to remove the massive load from the old girl.

Jeffery built a simple hydroelectric system on the two small creeks that flowed through the ranch he had purchased. The system provided valuable electricity, enabling him to speed up the mining and processing of the ore.

Figure 90-Much of the mining was done on the sheer vertical face

With the hydro-electric plant in place, the power and telephone poles, wire, and hardware had to be packed up the mountain to the mine. Mules were trained to transport poles around the switchbacks on the steep trail. It took careful training and ingenious rigging to get two mules tied together, one after the other, with two poles on their backs, to maneuver the switchbacks without pushing one another off the trail.

Cattle and produce were raised at the ranch to feed the miners and any surplus was sold off to help defray mining costs. The ranch became the all-inclusive base of operations for the new mine.

The mine may well have been one of the most scenic in the U.S. Looking to the west, the view took in the beautiful Chalfant and Owens Valleys and the soaring peaks of the Sierra Nevada crowned the scene like royalty.

The miners found the weather was just as dramatic. Even at 9,000', the sun would blaze warmly during the summer while deep snows often halted work during the winter. Lightning storms that would make Zeus envious were common and the miners would remove themselves from the metal bed frames and metal buildings during a storm. It was reported, "at times like these, the miners prayed a lot." Flash floods were another common occurrence at the mine, frequently washing out parts of its infrastructure.

A road was eventually built to the lower camp located at 7,500, but a mule trail remained the only access to the upper mine…1,500 feet higher up the mountain. Demand for sillimanite exploded during World War II, as the nation produced hundreds of thousands of pieces of equipment that required sparkplugs.

But by the late 1940s, an affordable synthetic was developed, and the demand for sillimanite quickly diminished. The Champion Sparkplug Mine soon closed. Dr. Jeffery's sparkplug mine played an important and vital role in securing the safety for our country, and powering automobiles along our nation's highways and of course…along El Camino Sierra as well.

Figure 91-The "upper camp" was constructed literally on the side of the cliff

CHAPTER THIRTYTWO

BASQUE OF THE EASTERN SIERRA

The raising of sheep in the Eastern Sierra has been taking place almost since the first Europeans arrived in the 1850s. The sheep not only provided a ready food source for the early miners and settlers, but their wool was highly prized for the production of clothing and other garments.

Caring for the sheep was a tough job. Working interminable hours, rarely taking a day off and enduring months of isolation caused many an American to pass on taking up sheepherding as a profession. But for the young men in the mountainous Basque regions of Spain and France, shepherding was a way to parlay a few years of hard work into a better life.

The first Basque to arrive in America tried their luck at panning for gold during the California gold rush. Most didn't strike it rich, and they quickly discovered they could make more money taking advantage of the plentiful rangelands of the American West, raising sheep to meet the great demand for fresh meat.

The Basques quickly developed an enduring reputation as the finest sheep men in the American West. Basque shepherds had an uncanny ability to find the richest pastures, rarely lost lambs to predators, and their ewes routinely had the most offspring.

The meadows and rangelands of the Eastern Sierras were particularly attractive to the Central Valley sheep ranchers. The ranchers and Basque sheepherders would move their flocks from the winter ranges of the Central Valley, to the tall grasses of the valleys and meadows east of the Sierra crest during the summer months.

It was one of the longest annual stock drives in the nation. To the south, the flocks traveled 400 miles over the Tehachapi Mountains to Mojave, then up past Lone Pine and Bishop to the high mountain meadows of the Sierra. The sheep men from the northern part of California were bringing their sheep over the lower Sierra passes to the Carson Valley of northern Nevada. The trips were reversed in the fall, though several Nevada ranchers established a permanent year round operation. As motorized equipment improved it became more cost effective for the sheep to be trucked back and forth between the Central Valley and the Eastern slope.

Figure 92-Basque sheepherder and his dogs

The first Basques brought their relatives and friends from their home villages in Spain and France, and soon there was a steady flow of shepherds to the sheep-growing regions of California, Nevada and Idaho.

Figure 93-Many Basque families from Europe joined their sheepherding relatives

Basques are proud of their heritage and boast of having the oldest surviving culture in Europe. Although their homeland straddles the mountains between Spain and France, they do not consider themselves to be part of either country. They inhabited the Pyrenees Mountains long before Spain and France became nations.

Figure 94-Basque sheepherders are regarded as the best in the world

But opportunity for the Basque was limited in the remote mountain villages of the Pyrenees, and by the turn of the century, large numbers of Basques were coming to the United States to find a new life. They quickly adapted to the hard life of sheepherding and proved themselves "natural sheep men," said Martin Etchamendy, a Central Valley sheep ranch owner. "Basques have an ability around sheep we haven't found with other people," said Etchamendy, who worked as a shepherd when he immigrated to America. "For centuries, people have been raising sheep in the Pyrenees.

Although not all Basques were shepherds in the old country, most had some sheep on their family farms. Ever since we were 4 or 5 years old, we have been caring for the sheep, herding them and helping make cheese from their milk."

The demanding work was also lonely, as the sheepherders would often spend months in the most remote and isolated spots. Not all the Basque were sheep men and some (especially those with families) built hotels and boarding houses to cater to the needs of the sheep men. These businesses became the focal point of Basque culture in their local communities, providing an opportunity to catch up on news from home, read Basque newspapers and enjoy a familiar meal at a large table in a family style setting.

Basque boardinghouses sprang up in a number of Nevada towns including Winnemucca, Elko, Reno and Gardnerville. Word began to spread of the great food served in a family style setting, and local residents began to patronize the new restaurants as well. Basque restaurants are still very popular in northern Nevada and continue to be a great resource for preserving local history and heritage.

Figure 95-Most Basque restaurants serve their fare "family style"

The nature of the work the Basque sheepherders performed was transient. Not only would they make the long trip from the Central Valley to the Eastern Sierra, they were continually moving from spot to spot in search of fresh forage for their flocks.

A staple in the diet of these nomadic travelers was a tasty and crusty bread. Often times the shepherd's only piece of cooking equipment was the simple Dutch Oven. Out of necessity, the Basque sheepherders became masters in baking their hardy bread in this rather simple cooking implement.

In 1903, the city of Bishop, California was home to a popular Main Street bakery owned by the Schochs family. Their huge stone ovens produced an assortment of delicious baked goods for their Owens Valley customers.

To save himself some time, a Basque sheepherder approached the Schochs family, to see if they would bake the bread dough he had prepared ...in their oven. The Schochs agreed, and the system worked so well, that other sheepherders soon were asking the Schochs to bake their bread dough in their great stone oven.

The Schochs soon told the sheepherders they would make the bread dough themselves as well as bake the bread for them. Other customers became interested in this new bread and were soon requesting the Schochs bake this new Basque sheepherder's bread for them. The bread became known simply as "sheepherder" bread and grew into the most popular item from the bakery.

Figure 96-Sheepherder Bread was first introduced to the Eastern Sierra by the Basque

Tourists traveling through Bishop learned of the delicious sheepherder bread and began taking loaves of it back to their homes in Southern California and Northern Nevada. The popularity of the bread grew far and wide. In 1938, as others tried to imitate the popular product, the Schochs registered the name "Original Sheepherder" bread to protect and ensure its quality as it continued to grow. In the 1950s, the Schat family bought the bakery from the Schochs and continued to grow the bakery. Today, people come from the world over to Erick Schat's Bakkery in Bishop to pick up a loaf of this delicious Eastern Sierra history (as well as a huge selection other baked goods). Hardworking Basque and original sheepherder bread ...landmarks that got their start here, along El Camino Sierra.

Figures 97 and 98 (below)-Basque sheepherders have been a part of the Eastern Sierra landscape for over 150 years. Lake Tahoe-above and Owens Valley-below

CHAPTER THIRTYTHREE

MAJOR LEAGUES IN THE HIGH SIERRA

Leo Durocher was a popular baseball player, coach and manager for the Brooklyn and later Los Angeles Dodgers, as well as other Major League Baseball teams from the 1930s into the 1960s. The "Lip" as Durocher was often known, was a fierce competitor. He knew how to win ball games, but he also excelled at stirring up trouble. His 95 career ejections from a game still ranks fourth among all baseball managers.

Durocher married Hollywood actress Laraine Day in 1947, just before she was to start filming the movie-*Tycoon* with co-star John Wayne. Much of the movie was to be filmed in the Alabama Hills near Lone Pine. According to a biography on John Wayne written by Maurice Zolotow…Wayne said that Durocher was the most openly jealous husband he had ever met. The "Lip" hovered on the set each day, making rude comments or glaring at Wayne whenever he and Day were filming romantic scenes. Ultimately, Wayne got so fed up with Durocher's suspicious ways, he ordered the set closed, the only time in his career he ever did so.

The reason Durocher had so much time on his hands during this period, lie in the fact he had been suspended from Major League Baseball for one season by the Commissioner, Hap Chandler. Durocher enjoyed cards and other "wagering" activities and had a number of acquaintances that "Black Sox" conscious baseball did not approve of. Durocher admitted having associated with a known gambler and Chandler placed him out of Major League Baseball action for one year. With not much to do while on suspension, Durocher came to Lone Pine with his movie actress wife while her scenes were being filmed.

Once John Wayne placed Durocher on suspension from the movie set, the Lip looked for other ways to keep himself busy. According to Bill Bauer, who was the Superintendent of Lone Pine Schools and its baseball coach at that time, Durocher became bored and started to really miss "the game" while hanging out in Lone Pine. He looked the high school coach up and volunteered to assist him in coaching the Lone Pine baseball team, as long as it was kept on the QT. Durocher was not permitted to have any association with baseball during his suspension and he didn't want to bring the wrath of Chandler down even harsher. A deal was struck, and baseball coach Bill Bauer and the Lone Pine Eagles had some very professional coaching assistance that year.

Figure 99-Leo Durocher was an unofficial coach of the Lone Pine High School baseball team during his suspension in 1947

It's lost to history whether Durocher's presence that year had any effect on the Lone Pine Eagles won-loss record…but the long-ago memory of a feisty major leaguer coaching Owens Valley kids in the shadow of Mt. Whitney…remains another little-known tale now told…along El Camino Sierra.

CHAPTER THIRTYFOUR

HOT...HOT...HOT!

The landscape of the Eastern Sierra is one of the most dramatic to be found. Highly active geologic actions have formed the high mountains and deep valleys, and many of these processes are still at work today. The earth's crust is relatively thin throughout the route of El Camno Sierra. The thin crust allows the magma from deep within the earth's core to rise close to and occasionally extrude through the surface of the earth, often creating hot springs. The Eastern Sierra is home to numerous geothermal areas, and it's claimed Nevada has more natural hot springs than any other state.

Many geothermal areas can be found in the land of Washoe and Tahoe. As is the case with most hot springs, Native Americans have enjoyed the relaxing waters long before the arrival of euro-settlers. The waters were not only used for relaxing soaks but often for food preparation as well. This tale is about three of the area's more popular hot springs that are still in use today.

STEAMBOAT HOT SPRINGS

In the area south of present-day Reno, pioneers headed for California during the 1840s made mention of "the columns of steam" seen as they made their way along the wagon trail to cross the Sierra Nevada Mountains.

Felix Monet filed claims on this land in 1860 and made plans to develop it. Over the next few years, cottages, a bath-house and even a hospital were built at the site for the comfort of guests. Mark Twain wrote in 1863 of a visit he made to Monet's new resort, "From one spring the boiling water is ejected a foot or more by the infernal force at work below, and in the vicinity of all of them one can hear a constant rumbling and surging, somewhat resembling the noises peculiar to a steamboat in motion-hence the name." Many other names were given to the hot springs, but Steamboat was the one that stuck.

Fire destroyed the complex, but it was rebuilt to an even grander scale in 1867 with a drugstore and 50-room hotel. The spa became very popular with miners, tourists and health seekers. The Virginia and Truckee

Railroad (V&T) built a train stop at the resort, and a dance hall and a few saloons were added. The Grand Hotel was built featuring elegant accommodations which played host to U.S. Senators, state Governors, wealthy mine owners from the Comstock and even President Ulysses S. Grant. The largest swimming pool in all of Nevada was built here at the corner of Highway 395 and the Mt. Rose Highway.

Figure 100-Steamboat Hot Springs south of Reno circa 1930s

Earthquakes would occasionally alter the flow of the springs. A wildland fire destroyed the resort again in 1901, but several smaller spas and hot spring facilities continued along Steamboat up until the late 1940s.

But the high heat of the pools and heavy mineral content of the volcanic waters eventually gave the owners too many problems and most all the Steamboat businesses and the pool, closed down. But that was not the end of the Steamboat geothermal area.

In 1986 Far West Electric Energy Funds Ltd. opened the first of what are now eight geothermal electrical facilities at Steamboat. The eight units produce enough electricity to meet the needs of 45,000 households a year. And if you're still interested in enjoying the warm historic waters of Steamboat Hot Springs, you have that opportunity at the Steamboat Hot Springs Healing Center & Spa which still operates there today.

CARSON HOT SPRINGS

Tucked away against the hills, a few miles northeast of the Nevada State Capital, lies the historic Carson Hot Springs. These soothing waters of pure enjoyment have also been frequented by Native Americans for hundreds of years. Virginia City prospectors made good use of the special warm waters while searching the hills and canyons of the Comstock.

Figure 101-"Worlds Finest Mineral Water"

In 1880, Thomas Swift purchased the property and built a clubhouse, a few bathhouses and a hotel where he charged $14 a week. Just two years later, James Shaw purchased the springs and shortly, built a "plunge" he claimed was the largest in the state. A few years later Shaw even began bottling and selling the special waters of the springs for its purported medicinal value.

The hot springs began to achieve a bit of celebrity status when in 1896, opera star Miss Gracie stayed at the resort followed the next year by prize fighter "Gentlemen Jim" Corbett, who stayed several weeks at the resort training for an upcoming fight in Carson City with Bob Fitzsimmons.

Business at the springs continued to grow. A road was built from town out to the resort and in 1910, it received the name Carson Hot Springs. A dance hall was built, and the sounds of big band music could be heard several nights a month.

Carson Hot Springs successfully flowed through the years with an occasional change in ownership and the water today still streams out of the ground at 121°F. The addition of mini spas compliments the soothing and warming outdoor pool and hot tubs. You'll even find a delightful eclectic restaurant to temp your palette and a new micro-brewery owned and operated by award winning brewers offers a tempting selection of fine ales and beverages.

WALLEYS HOT SPRINGS

In 1860, former New Yorkers David & Harriet Walley came upon an area of hot springs along the base of the Sierra Nevada Mountains just a bit south of the town of Genoa, Nevada's first settlement. The Walleys laid claim to the property, erected a tent and started charging passing travelers .50¢ for a bath.

In 1864, the Walleys gained clear title to their land and built a grand hotel with 40 bedrooms and 11 bathrooms. The resort included a livery stable, saloon, wine cellar, ballroom and beautiful vegetable and flower gardens.

Figure 102-Walley's Hot Spring Resort about 1915

The springs were promoted as "medicinal" and people flocked to Walley's to receive "the cure." Mark Twain and Ulysses S. Grant also visited the hot springs resort, and many Comstock miners found their way to Walleys' for a soak.

Walleys was sold several times over the next 100 years, and the name eventually changed to Genoa Hot Springs. Fires took their toll on the resort over the years, though it still continued on as an important part of the Carson Valley community. In 1952, Ginny and Halvor Smedsrud leased the resort, and operated a renowned gourmet restaurant there, the Bonanza Inn. Many longtime Carson Valley residents still hold special fond memories of their delightful times at the historic hot springs.

Over the years, Walleys Hot Springs Resort has evolved. The current owners have resurrected its original name, though David and Harriet probably wouldn't recognize the place. Luxury townhouse units overlook the idyllic Carson Valley at this destination spa resort. A gourmet restaurant pleases the most discerning palate and the property has designed a world class and exceptionally beautifully outdoor wedding and event venue. And most important…there's still plenty of warm relaxing water at the pool and soaking springs to help make a soak at David Walley's Resort an experience long to remember.

CHAPTER THIRTYFIVE

ALL SHOOK UP

May 18, 1980 was a monumental day in the history of the United States. After several months of bluster, a geologically young volcano in Washington State named Mt. St Helens, literally blew its top. The eruption removed 1,300' from the volcano's height, created monolithic dust clouds, flattened trees for hundreds of square miles and sent a pyroclastic flow of super-heated gas roaring down the mountain's slopes that in turn created a massive flow of mud and debris that destroyed structures 50 miles away. Fifty-seven people died in this cataclysmic event.

On May 25, only one week after Mt. St. Helen's eruption, an earthquake of magnitude 6.0 on the Richter Scale, struck the Long Valley Caldera just a few miles southeast of the town of Mammoth Lakes. This initial quake was followed in the next 48 hours by a swarm of magnitude 4.0 or larger quakes, including three more greater than 6.0. Startled geologists also noticed that the floor of Long Valley had risen a dramatic 10 inches during this period of seismic activity.

Damage from the earthquakes was most pronounced in the Mammoth and Crowley Lakes area. After the quake, Mammoth Lakes was without power for several hours. There was some damage to buildings including broken windows and water mains, cracked plaster and fallen chimneys. Stores and businesses reported extensive damage to shelf stock and many residents had personal contents in their home shaken to the floor.

The earth's rumblings in Mammoth were not a complete surprise. Geologists were well aware of the area's volcanic past. Mammoth Mountain is part of the shell of an ancient volcano and seismic activity had been observed in the area for decades. Initial damage losses to schools, public buildings and roads in the Mammoth Lakes area was estimated to be $2 million. Landslides and rockfalls occurred throughout the region, with one rockslide injuring two hikers in the nearby Yosemite back country. The rockslides created huge dust clouds in the mountain canyons after the larger quakes and cracks in the ground opened in numerous locations around Mammoth & Crowley Lakes

The earthquakes continued for three more days, though not as severe as the opening salvo. Due to the recent ruinous event that had occurred at Mt. St. Helens, geologists were alarmed at what was happening at Mammoth Lakes and the seismic activity received a good deal of press.

Figure 103-Several stores in Mammoth Lakes experienced extensive damage to the inventory on their shelves and a lesser extent to the structures themselves

Geologists brought in additional equipment to carefully monitor the earth movements. Swarms of earthquakes continued in the area on and off for the next two years and a lava dome continued to grow on the floor of Long Valley. Scientists, government officials, visitors and residents ...all held their collective breath.

On May 27 of 1982, as the earthquakes continued and the lava dome rose several more inches, federal geologists issued an official "notice of potential volcanic hazard." The warning came on the Friday of Memorial Day weekend and was broadcast widely on radio, television and in the print media. The serious warning from the USGS alarmed everyone. Mammoth visitors quickly canceled their holiday plans and even many residents of Mammoth Lakes left the area.

With the terrifying images of the recent Mt. St. Helens catastrophe still fresh in their minds, visitors continued to stay away from the Mammoth area. According to the town manager at the time, Mammoth Lakes' economy collapsed. In the next few years, housing prices were cut in half, dozens of business closed, stores stood empty and townspeople left to find work elsewhere.

The seismic activity and bad press did not relent. In early 1983, two magnitude 5.0 earthquakes struck, and the lava dome rose another three inches.

Concerned that the only road that led out of town for people to leave by should an evacuation become necessary, aimed straight towards the area of the greatest concern, officials built a second road which exited the town of Mammoth Lakes to the north. It was first referred to as the "escape route"...but tourism officials, already faced with the huge challenge of just getting people to not be afraid of visiting the area, were able to get the name changed to the less threatening "Scenic Loop Road."

Figure 104-The Mammoth Lakes Scenic Loop was first referred to as the "Escape Route"

Eventually, the seismic activity lessened, and the geologists withdrew their public warnings. Slowly, people regained confidence that all was safe and beautiful Mammoth Lakes slowly began to regain its former luster.

Evidence of Mammoth Lakes' active geologic past is still quite evident. The Mono Craters are just a few miles to the north. Earthquake Fault is a sizeable fissure clearly visible along the road to the Mammoth Ski Area and volcanic activity near Horseshoe Lake has intermittently caused high levels of CO_2 which in turn has killed numerous trees in the area and created a "ghost forest."

Overall, seismic activity around Mammoth Lakes has been rather light in recent years. If you are considering moving or visiting here, know that it appears this sublimely beautiful region is no more at risk than other area of the state. In a 2017 article from the U.S. Geological Survey, a geologist notes "the odds of an eruption occurring in any given year near Mammoth Lakes, are one in a few hundred, which are comparable to the odds for a great earthquake anywhere along the infamous San Andreas fault in California."

Figure 105-CO2 from volcanic activity has killed hundreds of trees at Horseshoe Lake

So, don't worry…stick around, because life is grand in the Eastern Sierra. And if you ever do find yourself out in the midst of a bit of a ground shaking occurrence…just head to the nearest stationary store…it's the safest place you'll find during any earthquake, here along El Camino Sierra.

Figure 106-Earthquake Fault can be viewed off the road to Mammoth Ski Area

CHAPTER THIRTYSIX

IN IT FOR THE LONG RUN

Many people are well familiar with the quaint community of Genoa, Nevada. Nestled at the base of the mighty Sierra Nevada Mountains just a bit southwest of Carson City, the historic town has many tales to tell. Genoa got its start in 1850, when a group of settlers established a trading post to serve the prospectors headed to the California goldfields. It became the first permanent settlement in Nevada and today is the Silver State's oldest town.

Figure 107-Genoa is Nevada's first and oldest town-founded 1850

It seems only fitting that the oldest town would also own title to at least a few other "oldest" claims. Right in the center of downtown Genoa is "Nevada's Oldest Thirst Parlor," the Genoa Bar.

The building was constructed in 1853 and was first known as Livingston's Exchange and a few years later as Fettic's Exchange. Fettic served fine wines, liquors and cigars, and promoted his business with an invitation, "I would be pleased to have all my old friends call and they would be treated in the most cordial manner."

Much of whatever has ever entered the bar is still there. The electric lights were originally oil burning and were converted when the electric company brought power to Genoa around the beginning of the 20th century. The ancient wood stove provides the saloon's only source of heat.

The Diamond Dust mirror on the back of the bar came from Glasgow, Scotland, in the late 1840's. Unbelievably, it was brought in a sailing ship around Cape Horn to San Francisco, then brought across the Sierra Nevada Mountains on a rutted trail in a covered wagon. It arrived without a scratch. If you shine a flashlight into the mirror, you can see the diamond dust reflecting the light.

Figure 108-The Genoa Bar's mirror was brought around Cape Horn in the 1840s

Bar patrons may notice a trap door near the pool table. The source of many far-fetched tales, the door leads to a cold storage area. Blocks of ice would be harvested during the winter months from two small lakes high above Genoa in the Carson Range. The ice was packed in burlap and straw, brought to the Genoa Bar and stored below ground for use during the year.

For such a small bar and a bit off the beaten path, the Genoa Bar can boast a long list of A-Listers as its former patrons. Mark Twain enjoyed a beverage here when he first reported for the Territorial Enterprise which opened in Genoa before moving to Virginia City. Presidents Ulysses S. Grant and Theodore "Teddy" Roosevelt enjoyed a refreshing drink on a visit to the area. Carol Lombard and Clark Gable came here to play high stakes poker games with the local cattle barons. Among the other famous and infamous, Lauren Bacall, Richard Boone, Ronnie Howard, Red

Skelton and Cliff Robertson, as well as all Nevada Governors have come through its doors.

The Genoa Bar has provided a perfect backdrop for scenes in a number of Hollywood movies. *The Shootist* with John Wayne, *Charley Varrick* with Walter Matthau and Joe Don Baker, *Honky Tonk Man* with Clint Eastwood and *Misery* with James Cann and Kathy Bates to name just a few.

According to current owner Lindsey Mcinnerney, when filming of the Carson Valley scenes for the *Shootist* were finished up, John Wayne came in and asked the bar keep what the highest grossing day of the year was for the bar. The bartender replied with his answer and Wayne said "times that by seven and I want the keys and I don't want anyone coming in."

Figure 109-John Wayne rented the entire Genoa Bar for a week once filming for the movie-*The Shootist* finished up

Big name musicians have also found their way to the Genoa Bar. Willie Nelson, Charlie Daniels, Merle Haggard, Waylon Jennings, Johnny Cash, Slim Pickens, John Denver, and former Lake Tahoe residents Captain and Tennille have all enjoyed a beverage or two and possibly a song at the oldest Nevada thirst parlor.

Today, the bar enjoys a brisk tourist business and continues to be a favorite with locals as well. It still is considered the unofficial community gathering place.

On a side note, if you've never been to Genoa, mark it down on your bucket list of places to visit. The State of Nevada operates the Mormon Station State Park. The Douglas County Courthouse Museum is one of the finest small-town museums you will find and every year on the last full weekend of September, the town hosts the famous Candy Dance.

The Genoa "Candy Dance" originated in 1919 as an effort to raise money to purchase street lights for the small, but enterprising community. Lillian Virgin Finnegan, daughter of then prominent Judge Daniel Webster, suggested the idea of a dance to raise money, and making candy to pass around during the dance as an incentive for a good "turn-out" of couples. The "Dance" is now a two-day affair, featuring not only some two-stepping and strutting, but dinner, live music, a craft show and much more.

It's comforting to know that in an era where businesses often come and go with the frequency of the changing of the seasons, that in Nevada's oldest town...some things continue to stay quite the same.

Figure 110-The Genoa Bar (left), Nevada's oldest "thirst parlor"

CHAPTER THIRTYSEVEN

SHRIMP PLATE?

If you talk to a chef at most any nice restaurant, they'll tell you shrimp is one of the most popular items on their menu. Many a traveler on El Camino Sierra is a big fan of the tasty crustacean.

Here in the Eastern Sierra is a species of shrimp that probably won't excite many culinary experts, but its haute cuisine to thousands of migratory birds that make their fast food stop at scenic Mono Lake.

Ancient Mono Lake is home to a species of brine shrimp known as *Artemia Monica*, which is found nowhere else in the world. The brine shrimp is an important food source for eared grebes, Wilson's phalaropes and California gulls when these species are present at Mono Lake.

Figure 111-Brine shrimp are a primary food source for the California Gulls that frequent Mono Lake

An estimated 4-6 trillion brine shrimp inhabit Mono Lake during the warmer summer months. They live for up to 6 months and produce two to three generations a year. As the water cools when winter nears, the shrimp produce eggs and then die. In the spring, the eggs hatch and the first brine shrimp adults appear in mid-May. Biologists have found 50,000 shrimp in a single cubic yard of Mono Lake water.

The brine shrimp are also an important industry in the lightly populated Mono Basin. The tiny shrimp have been harvested commercially at Mono Lake since the 1950s, with the operation located on the west shore of Mono Lake. The local family owned lakeside production facility consists of harvesting boats, a processing plant, sub-zero freezing equipment and storage facilities. Mono Lake brine shrimp are harvested live, rinsed with fresh water, sealed in plastic bags and flash frozen.

Figure 112-Up to 50,000 brine shrimp live in one cubic yard of Mono Lake water

Who eats the processed brine shrimp? Commercial shrimp hatcheries and farms use the Mono Lake brine shrimp the world over for feed. The shrimp has also been used as food for aquarium fish. Recent annual harvests have been as high as 450,000 pounds. The shrimp population appears to be unaffected by either bird predation or commercial harvest.

Resist the urge to make a joke to your food server next time you dine at one of the Eastern Sierra's many fine restaurants. You just never know what you might be served...if you order the shrimp plate...here along El Camino Sierra.

CHAPTER THIRTYEIGHT

GHOSTS RIDERS IN THE SKY

For this next tale, we take the liberty of detouring several miles east of the Eastern Sierra region to the arid landscapes of Death Valley National Park. Though a hundred miles or so distant, Death Valley will forever be intricately linked to the area found in the shadows of the Sierra Nevada Mountains. Afterall, you can see Mt. Whitney from Dantes View right? Plus…we just really like this particular tale.

Ghost Riders in the Sky is arguably one of the most recognizable and popular western songs ever recorded. The Western Writers of America Association include it in their list of top 100 western songs of all time.

More than 50 different artists have recorded the 1948 classic, including Burl Ives, Marty Robbins, Vaughn Monroe, Johnny Cash, Gene Autry and the Sons of the Pioneers. Lawrence Welk and his orchestra did an instrumental version in 1961, and even crooner Bing Crosby recorded his version in 1949. Bing's version actually made it to number 16 on the Billboard charts! So, what's the tie between *Ghost Riders in the Sky* and Eastern California?

National Park Service Ranger Stan Jones was transferred from the cool glacier meadows of Mt. Rainer National Park, to the searing heat of a Death Valley summer in July of 1945. Jones occupied his off time in the lonely expanses of Death Valley, strumming his old Martin guitar and writing music. Jones recounted how once, while watching a turbulent summer storm from the porch of the Emigrant Ranger station, the wind shredded clouds reminded Jones of a ghost story he was told by an old cowboy when he was only twelve years old. Jones said it was from this storm and old tale, the lyrics for *Ghost Riders in the Sky* was born.

One of Jones's duties in Death Valley was to act as the Park Service liaison to the movie studios when they came to Death Valley to film. In the evenings, Jones would often entertain the Hollywood crew with songs he wrote and sang, including *Ghost Riders in the Sky*.

Encouraged by actor Randolph Scott, Jones went to Los Angeles on his vacation in 1948 to try and sell some of the music he wrote. RCA picked up a few of Jones's songs, including *Ghost Riders in the Sky,* and by April of 1949, Jones's Death Valley inspired song had become one of the most popular in the entire country.

Figure 113-Stan Jones "The Singing Ranger

Jones soon left the National Park Service to start a new career. Jones was hired as a technical advisor to the filming of *The Walking Hills,* where he met and befriended director John Ford, who helped open the door to his new career.

For the next 14 years, Jones worked as a song writer, musician and even landed a few acting rolls in Hollywood. Jones wrote almost entirely Western music during his songwriting career. He composed songs for several Western movies by Ford and other directors including *The Searchers* and *Rio Grande.* He also played small parts in several Western films.

In 1955 Jones began writing for the Disney Studios. He was co-writer of the theme song for the television series *Cheyenne,* and in 1956 was hired to play Deputy Harry Olson in the syndicated television series *Sheriff of Cochise* (1956–1958). Jones had acting roles in two additional Disney films.

In 1958, at the request of the National Park Service and with the backing of Disney Studios, Jones wrote and produced the album *Songs of the*

National Parks featuring Stan Jones and "the Ranger Chorus." The LP featured favorites such as *Along the Yellowstone*, *Ranger Hymn* and *Grand Canyon*.

Figure 114-Jones made an album, *Songs of the National Parks* for Walt Disney Company featuring backup vocals by the "Ranger Chorus"

Two other Jones's songs, the theme from *The Searchers*, and *Cowpoke* were also chosen by members of the Western Writers of America as being among the Top 100 Western songs of all time.

But for those of us here listening in to some old western music on the radio as we motor along El Camino Sierra…we'll always remember Jones as the Death Valley Ranger…who in that fierce desert storm could see…*Ghost Riders in the Sky.*

UNIVERSITY NEVADA RENO

In addition to being Nevada's oldest institution of higher education, UNR also boasts 11 diverse museums, galleries and attractions dedicated to furthering the cultural education of Northern Nevada.
Visit their website for a complete
list of all attractions in their Museum District
www.unr.edu

CHAPTER THIRTYNINE

RENO'S LEVI LEGACY

Jacob Youphes was born in 1831 in the Russian port city of Riga, now the capital of Latvia. Jacob immigrated to the United States at the age of 23 and changed his surname to Davis.

Jacob Davis learned the tailoring business working at shops in New York, Maine, and northern California. He tried his luck at prospecting for gold on the Fraser River in Canada and sold tobacco and wholesale pork in Virginia City. In 1868, Jacob decided to settle down in Reno, Nevada, where he first partnered up with Frederick Hertlein to build the Reno Brewing Company. Davis soon moved on to other ventures.

Figure 115-Jacob Davis (left) of Reno, created the idea of using rivets on the seams of denim to make the durable pants we now call jeans. Levi Strauss is on the right

Relying on his skills as a tailor, Davis turned to making tents, horse blankets, and other outdoor supplies for the surveyors and teamsters of the Central Pacific Railroad, who were laying track for the transcontinental railroad across Nevada. Davis favored a heavyweight blue denim material and a ten-ounce white duck twill for most of his custom work. He bought his fabric from a San Francisco wholesaler named Levi Strauss.

Tired of what seemed like continual repair of her husband's work pants, a miner's wife came into Davis's shop in December 1870 looking for help. The miner's wife asked Davis to make an extra sturdy pair of pants for her husband. Using the duck cloth and denim, Davis added copper rivets to the seams of his custom pants for added strength. The wife was delighted.

Davis's idea was a good one. Word of the new creation spread like wildfire among the area miners and laborers. Davis was overwhelmed with orders for his sturdy riveted pants. Realizing that he needed a business partner to help finance his new idea, he approached his supplier Levi Strauss. On May 20, 1873, Jacob W. Davis and Levi Strauss & Company were issued patent #139121 for copper-riveted pants. That same year, Davis added an orange-threaded double arc design to the rear pockets of his pants to distinguish them from the work of competitors.

Figure 116-Some historians credit Reno's Jacob Davis's creation of the durable, riveted denim jeans for playing a large role in the winning of the west

The patent for Davis's riveted pants was granted and Davis sold his Reno tailor shop and moved his family to San Francisco. He supervised the manufacture of his new durable trousers at the Levi Strauss factory which worked around the clock to keep up with the demand. The Levi factory employed up to 450 people. The company broadened its product line, producing a variety of riveted denim clothing.

Davis's copper-riveted sensation is arguably one of the most enduring Nevada-based inventions in the Silver State's history.

CHAPTER FORTY

LON CHENEY'S CABIN

Born to deaf parents in Colorado in 1883, actor Lon Cheney Sr. was a master of pantomime on the big screen during the silent-film era. He played numerous supporting roles until *The Miracle Man* (1919) made him a star. Known as the "Man of a Thousand Faces," Cheney was famous for his ability to transform himself through the special use of makeup which he developed. He often played grotesque characters in films including *The Unholy Three*. He is best known for his performances in *The Hunchback of Notre Dame* and *The Phantom of the Opera*.

Figure 117-Cheney In Phantom of the Opera

In a 1925 issue of Movie Magazine, Cheney dismissed his amazing ability to transform himself into the first cinema vampire, the hunchback Quasimodo, or hundred-year-old villain Mr. Wu using only makeup and body movement as mere "extraordinary characterization." In truth, Cheney's talent helped propel him into a true Hollywood super-star. But acting wasn't Cheney's only passion. Growing up in Colorado as a young boy, Cheney enjoyed any outoor adevnture and was quite a skilled fisherman. He would take numerous camping vacation trips to the Eastern Sierra Nevada, spending weeks at a time enjoying the creeks, mountains and invigorating air.

He longed to be able to enjoy more time in the mountains and dreamed of a cabin in the High Sierra. His dream eventually became a reality. Obtaining a special use permit from the United States Forest Service, Cheney was granted permission to construct a mountain cabin on the banks of Big Pine Creek. The site was where Cheney had camped and fished for years. At that time (1929), it was one and a half miles from the nearest road creating some signifecent logisticial challenges.

Cheney contracted with famous Southern California architect Paul R. Williams to design his vacation home. Williams was known as the "architect of the celebrities," having designed homes for Frank Sinatra, Lucille Ball and Desi Arnaz, Barbara Stanwyck and Charles Correll. The busy movie star thought his rustic home in the wilderness was paradise. Cheney exclaimed, "Tonight I start out for the High Sierra. No shaving, no makeup, no interviews for four long, lazy weeks. We sleep under the pines and I try to climb high enough to reach the snows."

The 1,288-square-foot granite fieldstone building, now with a corrugated metal roof cost $12,000 to build. The building had two-foot thick walls, a gabled roof and kerosene lamp lighting. Though the interior was simple, consisting of one large living room and a separate kitchen, it had a number of William's touches—a large granite fireplace, tongue-in-groove pine flooring and amazing views of the canyon and Big Pine Creek. The orientation of the building ensured that the views became an important design element. Unfortunately, Cheney spent only a few months at his cabin, dying in August, 1930 within a short time of its completion.

The building was sold in 1932 and again in 1955. In 1980, after the special use permit expired, the structure became government property. For a number of years the Forest Service examined different uses for the cabin and even considered demolition. But once the engineers did their calculations, they realized that the amount of dynamite needed to destroy the granite structure would cause more damage to the environment than letting it stay.

Today, hikers may appreciate the masterful work of this backcountry beauty from the outside as they hike the trail in Big Pine Canyon. Please be respectful that the interior of the cabin remains closed and off limits.

Figure 118-Lon Cheney's cabin has granite walls two-feet thick

CHAPTER FORTYONE

ACCIDENTAL PRESERVATION

Lake Tahoe is among the brightest jewels in the crown of mother nature, while at the same time one of the most heavily visited destinations in California. Development at certain parts of the lake resembles a bustling metropolis more than a mountain village.

Thankfully though, large portions of Lake Tahoe do remain undeveloped. Primarily on the northeast and southwest shores, the U.S. Forest Service, and the Nevada and California State Park systems manage thousands of acres of near pristine Lake Tahoe beauty.

The eight miles of Lake Tahoe shoreline between Sand Harbor and Glenbrook, remains "almost" completely without development. It is the largest stretch of unspoiled lakefront at "Big Blue." How did such a large tract of some of the most valuable real estate imaginable remain unspoiled? Can we thank Pa Cartwright and the boys for keeping this region, once known (at least in TV land) as the Ponderosa unsullied?

Not quite. Though the fictitious property did indeed appear on studio maps in the exact location on Tahoe's NE shore, the story of the untrampled lands of Lake Tahoe is so bizarre, even the best TV script writers couldn't top this one.

Figure 119-Map of TV's Bonanza's Ponderosa Ranch

Figure 120-George "Captain" Whittell

George Whittell Jr. was born in San Francisco in 1881, an heir to one of San Francisco's wealthiest families. His father was the founder of PG&E, the Northern California utility corporation, and owned many other businesses as well. George received his father's inheritance when the elder passed away in 1922. The estate was worth $29 million (about $35 billion in today's dollars). George was smart and shrewd. He nearly doubled the value of the estate and liquidated his stock holdings just before the 1929 stock market crash, becoming one of California's richest residents at age 49.

"Captain" Whittell, as he liked to be called, is quoted as saying: "When men stop boozing, womanizing and gambling, the bloom is off the rose." Whittell began his oppositional antics at quite an early age, running away with the Barnum & Bailey circus after high school rather than attending college, eloping with a chorus girl rather than marrying the society bride his parents had selected for him and buying himself a position in the Italian Army rather than waiting for the U.S. to join World War I.

The Whittell estate was located on the hills above San Francisco in an area now known as Woodside. In 1936, feeling threatened by California's tax and estate laws, Whittell decided to become a Nevada resident. He purchased twenty-seven miles of Lake Tahoe shoreline and nearly 40,000 total acres, mostly from the Carson and Tahoe Lumber and Fluming Company. It encompassed essentially 95% of the Nevada shoreline of Lake Tahoe—all the land that included Crystal Bay, Incline Village, Sand Harbor, Glenbrook, Cave Rock, Zephyr Cove and Round Hill. Whittell paid approximately $2.7 million or $81.00 per acre. For the remainder of his life, Whittell continued to acquire additional Lake Tahoe property.

Whittell quickly began work on his lakefront residence, which he named Thunderbird Lodge. Hiring renowned architect Frederic DeLongchamps from Reno for the design, Whittell's stone house was completed in 30 months. The estate included numerous small buildings but the house itself had no guest rooms, as Whittell didn't want overnight visitors.

The estate also included a card house, caretaker's cottage, a house for the help, an Admiral's House, boathouse with an adjoining 600-foot tunnel leading to the main house, a gatehouse, and the "Elephant House"—home to Mingo, Whittell's two-ton pet Indian Elephant. The large boathouse housed his custom 55-foot long mahogany and stainless-steel yacht, the Thunderbird.

Figure 121-Thunderbird Estate has a commanding view of Lake Tahoe

Early on, Whittell had plans for some major developments on his Lake Tahoe property, including casinos at Zephyr Cove and Sand Harbor. But as the years passed, he grew reclusive and favored his secluded hideaway and lifestyle. All plans for commercial development of his property faded. He continued to entertain friends including neighbor and former baseball great and part time Tahoe resident Ty Cobb, as well as fellow eccentric recluse Howard Hughes.

In addition to Mingo the elephant, Whittell began to amass a large animal collection, some brought back with him from African adventures including tigers, a giraffe, a bear and many more. A lion cub named Bill was one of

Whittell's favorite companions, and it often rode along with him in his cars. A car collector, who had later bought one of Whittell's classic Duesenbergs recalls, "It had scratches on the seat. He used to let this 300-pound lion sit shotgun with him, and its claws would come out and put holes in the seat."

He referred to his three aircraft as the "Whittell Airforce." There was a DC2 that served as his domestic, luxury aircraft in which he flew friends to boxing matches across the country and on social junkets. He had an amphibious airplane, the Grumman Goose, that he used to fly between the Bay Area and his Lake Tahoe home, and he sold his interest in a 307 Stratoliner when he learned it couldn't fly nonstop from the West Coast to Europe.

Figure 122-Whittell with one his "pets" he kept at his residence

But without a doubt, his pride and joy was his boat, the Thunderbird, a 55-foot, mahogany and stainless-steel, twin-V12-powered marvel. Designed by famed naval architect John L. Hacker, it was built by Huskins Boat Works in Bay City, Michigan at a cost of $87,000—about $1.5 million today. The boat is a one-off streamline modern masterpiece, and it looks like a burnished, wooden, floating Miami Beach hotel.

Whittell's health began to decline and he spent less and less time at his Lake Tahoe estate. He passed away in 1969 with his third wife Elia by his side.

Whittell's property was bought by an investor who soon sold most of the land to the U.S. Forest Service and Nevada State Parks. Thunderbird Lodge became part of a three-way land exchange, which conveyed the historic home to the non-profit Thunderbird Lodge Preservation Society. The TLPS does a masterful job in maintaining the home and the property, offering tours and special events by reservation during the summer.

Eccentric Lake Tahoe resident George Whittell. Though his refusal to pursue development of the 27 miles of shoreline he owned was more from his desire for privacy and seclusion, rather than intentional conservation, we can indisputably thank the good Captain for the natural and unspoiled beauty of Lake Tahoe's present-day eastern shoreline.

Figure 123-Whittell's personal boat was also dubbed the Thunderbird
Figure 124-Tours of Thunderbird Estate are available during the summer

TAKE A SENTIMENTAL JOURNEY WITH THESE OTHER FINE BOOKS FROM EL CAMINO SIERRA PUBLISHING

An Eastern Sierra Best Seller (our first volume)

The History of Furnace Creek Resort

A History of the Mt. Whitney Fish Hatchery

Retail and wholesale available
Quantity discounts   *www.elcaminosierra395.com*
Email us at   elcaminsosierra395@gmail.com

While traveling in the Eastern Sierra-listen in on 92.5 FM

Stream live at **https://www.sierrawave.net/tales-along-el-camino-sierra/**

CHAPTER FORTYTWO

CHUCK YEAGER SIERRA STORIES

Test pilot Chuck Yeager showed he had the "Right Stuff" throughout his storied career. Not only was he the first man to fly faster than the speed of sound, Yeager is credited with having flown more than 200 different types of aircraft. He was also an "Ace," having shot down 14 enemy planes during World War II.

Yeager loved the outdoors, and nothing could come between him and his annual two-week fishing treks into the High Sierra each July. Yeager's personal favorite catch? The golden trout, which he extolled as one of the best game fish and best eating fish to be found.

When the conversation turned to fishing, Yaeger would often produce a well-thumbed pack of color prints: The fish, some up to four and a half pounds, were the color of pure gold. Yeager's blue eyes would sparkle as he told and retold his favorite fish story.

In Yeager's 1984 autobiography, he reminisces about what he calls "Operation Golden Trout." Yeager and Air Force General Irving Branch had been enjoying beverages in the officer's club at Edwards Air Force base and after a few hours of relaxing, the two decided to go on their High Sierra fishing trip via helicopter instead of by foot. Yaeger and the general got dropped off by a Bell Aircraft HU-1 Huey helicopter flown by an Army Aviation Major with all their camping and fishing equipment at Yaeger's favorite Sierra lake.

Fishing was good and the congenial Yaeger invited two backpackers he had met, to fly out with him and the general when the helicopter came back to pick them up. But with four passengers instead of two, plus all the golden trout caught...the weight was more than the chopper could lift and it crashed into the lake. Fortunately, Chuck and the party escaped without serious injury. The group hiked out and the general sent a recovery team back to salvage what they could of the whirlybird.

Yeager would usually backpack into his High Sierra fishing trip. The strenuous trip would cripple many a younger man. "Years ago, when I was flying over the Mount Whitney area" Yeager said, "I spotted this lake way

up in the High Sierra—gin-clear and teeming with trout, up there above the timberline. Lake at 13,000 feet and the golden trout spawn in there. We packed in on foot…25 miles each way."

"When you really stop to think about it," Yeager said, "finding that lake like that, just with the luck of the flight pattern, that's one of the real rewards of flying. Those trout up there—they've got the real "Right Stuff." And so did Chuck Yeager. Whether flying at supersonic speed or angling for the legendary golden trout …here in the sparkling clear waters along El Camino Sierra.

Figures 125 & 126 (below)-Chuck Yeager…avid angler and American hero

CHAPTER FORTYTHREE
SPRINGS OF SURVIVAL

The grievous tale of the forlorn pioneers who nearly lost their lives in the daunting reaches of Death Valley is well known. Nearly 100 men, women and even children, came close to meeting their mortal fate while seeking a shortcut to the promises of riches they had hoped to find in the Sierra Nevada foothills during the California Gold Rush.

As food ran out and water became more difficult to find, the group split up into several smaller parties, with an "every man (and woman) for themselves" approach in trying to save their lives. One of the groups known as the Jayhawkers, abandoned their wagons, slaughtered most of their oxen and fought their way along an arid and terrible route. Water was very scare and often undrinkable when found. After five days of desperate searching with no good water, a party led by Ed Doty, found first damp ground and then a pool of good drinkable water on the divide where a great desert plain met the base of taller mountains.

Doty credited this water with saving the lives of his group. "We had been without water for five days," said Doty…"and came near starving to death, for it was impossible to swallow food when one becomes so desperately thirsty." Over the next few days, this same spring would be the salvation of others from the Death Valley party who were fortuitous enough to stumble upon it in their search for help.

During the next few decades, the springs came to be known as Indian Wells Springs, and became an important waypoint, providing a reliable source of fresh water for locals and passerby. In the 1860s, the Army maintained a small outpost at the site. Later, the main route from the Owens Valley to Southern California went right past these springs. A way-station was built that served the needs of the passing freighters who hauled silver and supplies between Los Angeles and the Cerro Gordo mines near Lone Pine. In the early 1900s, a small resort was developed espousing the curative powers of its "healing" waters, and the Civilian Conservation Corps operated out of a camp that was set up near the artesian well in the 1930s. A small settlement by the name of Homestead sprouted up around the area of the springs.

In 1960, a local family built a restaurant, Indian Wells Lodge, which has become a very popular Ridgecrest area eatery. In 1995, Indian Wells Brewery was born in one of the rooms at the restaurant. The brewery has used the historic waters of Indian Wells Spring to make their fine ales, lagers and pilsners and has grown into a 10,000 square foot facility. It has also has expanded to create a line of specialty soft drinks that also use the waters of historic Indian Wells Springs.

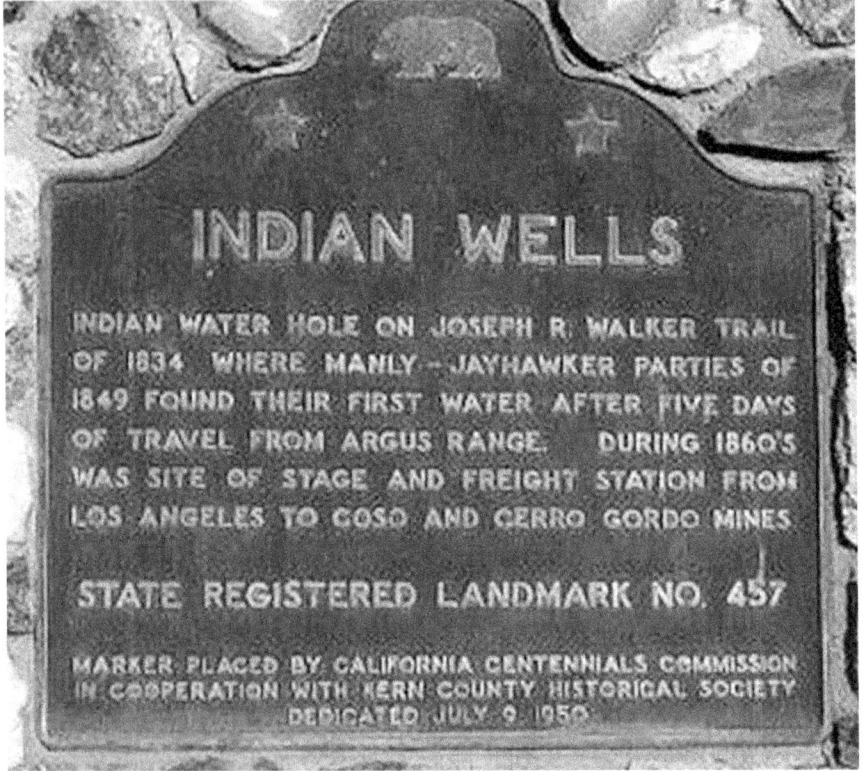

Figure 125 A-The state historical marker at Indian Wells Springs

If you would like to enjoy an important part of Eastern Sierra history, take a few minutes and stop by Indian Wells on your next trip along El Camino Sierra. Read the plaque denoting the important history…and look out over the vast expanse of Mojave Desert, and think back of the many brave and determined people who have depended on this historic watering hole for their livelihood…as well as their lives. Amongst all of the growth and change in our world, one thing has never changed though, travelers are always welcome to stop, rest, and enjoy everything the historic site has to offer.

BIBLIOGRAPHY

Chpt 1-Eastern California Museum files
Chpt 2-visitcarsonvalley.org, Wikipedia.org
Chpt 3-The Album, Times and Tales of Inyo-Mono Volume VI # 1, Eddie Ford
Chpt 4-Wikipedia.org, Mono County Museum files
Chpt 5-Eastern California Museum files
Chpt 6-Wikipedia.org, Silver Lake Resort
Chpt 7-nevadaart.org, americanart.si.edu, rissoliusa.com,
Chpt 8-Mono County Museum file
Chpt 9-Manzanar National Historic Site, Nikkei for Civil Rights & Redress
Chpt 10-Reno Historical Society, University of Nevada, Reno,
Chpt 11- The Album, Times and Tales of Inyo-Mono Vol 1 #3, Dave Babb
Chpt 12-Man from Mono, Lily Mathieu LaBraque
Chpt 13-Carson City Now, Kelsey Penrose; Legends of America, Kathy Weiser
Chpt 14-Nellie of Lundy, Nellie Bly O'Bryan; The Album, Times and Tales of Inyo-Mono Vol 5 # 3 Barbara Moore
Chpt 15-Wikipedia; National Register of Historic Places Nomination Form; Bentley Heritage LLC
Chpt 16-Saga of Inyo County, Leslie B. Hancock
Chpt 17-Eastern California Museum Files; Richard White oral history
Chpt 18-Saga of Lake Tahoe, E.B. Scott; Water Supply for the Comstock USGS, 1979 Hugh Shamberger
Chpt 19-Pearsonville, CA 93527, Janice Pearson
Chpt 20-Museum of Western Film History, Lone Pine
Chpt 21-www.airfields-freeman.com; www.militarymuseum.org
Chpt 22-Las Vegas Review Journal, 1/12/12, Ed Vogel; Nevada Appeal, 2/8/17, Dennis Cassinelli; Wikipedia.org
Chpt 23-Old Mammoth, Adele Reed
Chpt 24-www.29palms.marines.mil; www.mca-marines.org
Chpt 25-www.usmint.gov; nvculture.org
Chpt 26- The Album, Times and Tales of Inyo-Mono, Vol VI #1 & 2, Bill & Louise Kelsey
Chpt 27-Toms Place Resort, Eastern California Museum files
Chpt 28- LA Curbed 5/14/13, Adrian Kudler; The Sheet 10/28/17, Giles
Chpt 29-Nevada State Preservation Society, www.casino.org, David Sheldon
Chpt 30-Wikipedia.org; www.imdb.com; Carole Lester
Chpt 31- The Album, Times and Tales of Inyo-Mono Vol V #4, Bill & Louise Kelley; Mountain Mouse Land, Greg Wilkerson

Chpt 32-Smithsonian, "The Sheepmen, Hal Roth; www.knowledgecenter.unr.edu; Erick Schat oral history
Chpt 33-Museum of Western Film History, Chris Langley
Chpt 34-Visit Reno, Steamboat Springs, John Evanoff; Wikipedia.org; Carson Hot Springs; Travel Nevada, The Record Courier 12/19/02, Linda Hiller; www.david-walley.com
Chpt 35-USGS Fact Sheet 108-96; California Geology Vol 33 #9, Richard McJunkin & Trina Bedrossian; NY Times 9/11/02 Sandra Blakeslee
Chpt 36-Genoa Bar; KOLO Reno TV 1/30/19 Ben Deach
Chpt 37-Wikipedia.org; LA Times 10/12/04, David Lukas
Chpt 38-Ghost Riders in the Sky: The Life of Stan Jones, the Singing Ranger, Mike Ward
Chpt 39-Reno Historical Society; Culture Trip 8/4/2016, Courtney Holcomb
Chpt 40-www.paulreverewilliams.com; LA Times 6/7/2003, Leslie Carlson
Chpt 41-www.thunderbirdtahoe.org; www.onlinenevada.org; autoweek.com 11/10/17, Brett Berk
Chpt 42-Yeager: An Autobiography; www.outdoorlife.com 7/1/15, James Hall
Chpt 43-Death Valley in 49, Indian Wells Brewery

IMAGES

Referenced by photo Figure Number except where noted
California Department of Transportation vi
Author's Collection 15, 24, 26, 37, 46, 55, 56, 59, 78, 87, 89, 103, 104, 105, 106, 108, 114, 116, 118, 119, 125A and page iii
Eastern California Museum, photos by Burton Frasher 17, 18, 23, 25, 98, 111 and page viii top
Eastern California Museum 1,2,3,4,5,9,10,12,14,16, 34, 48, 49, 64, 65, 66, 67, 68, 72, 73, 74, 75, 76, 77, 79, 80, 92, 93, 94, 96 and pages vii bottom and 86
Douglas County Historical Society 6   Architecture.org 7
The Daily Gazette 8,   http://brbl-archive.library.yale.edu 22
moma.org 19,20,21,   Manzanar NHS 27,28,29
University of Nevada Online Digital Collections 30, 31, 32, 38, 42, 43, 44, 45, 52, 53, 54, 69, 70, 71, 97, 100, 102, 107, 120, 121, 122, 123, 124 and page 138
ballparkdigest.com 33   neitshade5.wordpress.com 35
commons.wikimedia.org 36   doctormacro.com 39

Mono Basin Historical Society 40,41
Mary Roper 50
Western Film History Museum 58
airfields-freeman.com-Jed Keck 60, 62
pexels.com 63,99,117
Betonbabe 82
Comic-mint.com 86
Smithsonian Magazine 95
Wikipedia 112
Bolid'Ster 115
Carson Hot Springs 101

Bentley Heritage LLC 47
mccunecollection.org 51
imdb.com 57, 109
Lockheed-Martin 61
Cultural Landscape Foundation 81
Nevada State Prison Preservation Society 83,84,85
The Album October 1992 88, 90, 91
Canyon Country Zephyr 110
Mike Ward 113
chuckyeager.com 125, 126

Front Cover and Back Cover University of Nevada, Reno Libraries' Digital Archive

We would love to hear from you!

If you have a comment you would like to send us, please do so! You can reach us at:

elcaminosierra395@gmail.com
or
Woodruff   1326 Kimmerling Rd # A   Gardnerville, NV 89460

Thank you and we hope you have enjoyed…
Tales Along El Camino Sierra Two!

www.ingramcontent.com/pod-product-compliance
Lightning Source LLC
Chambersburg PA
CBHW071403290426
44108CB00014B/1661